Double Double Your Money

Saving & Investing Ideas for Young Canadians & Their Parents

Paul F. Walsh

Double Double Your Money

ISBN: 9798386692858

DEDICATION

For my kids

Double Double Your Money

DISCLAIMER

This book is offered for entertainment purposes only. I am not a professional advisor in any capacity & none of the contents should be considered investing, financial planning, real estate, tax, marital, or legal advice. None of the investments mentioned should be taken as recommendations & I may, or may not, hold any of them in my own portfolio. The information & calculations provided here may be inaccurate, verify all information & calculations independently. Investing carries risk, consult an appropriate professional before making any decisions relating to investing, financial planning, real estate, matters of taxation, & legal matters.

Double Double Your Money

Table of Contents

Introduction

Do you know that a kid saving & investing the equivalent of a couple of hours pay a week could be a millionaire by retirement day? And that's a kid making minimum wage. My Mom & Dad didn't know this. I never learned about saving & investing 'til I was much older. Then I learned the hard way, making one mistake after another. Though I lost a few dollars & a few nights sleep along the way, I have learned enough to tilt the odds a little more in my favour now. While investing always comes with risk, not investing comes with risk too. Inflation evaporates the value of cash & bank interest rates won't compensate for that. I started my wealth-building journey late & I want my kids to begin theirs sooner.

The biggest advantage kids have is time. The biggest disadvantage kids have is thinking they have plenty of time. The difference time makes can be big. Really big. Most of us aren't brought up to think of saving **and investing** as a regular part of life. Sure, we might save for a bike when we're young. And for college or university as we get older. Then for a down payment on a home. But really, how many Moms & Dads can engage their kids with a conversation about retirement? About making a financial plan that covers a future so far away that it's almost unimaginable. When I was a kid, I would have preferred to watch grass grow. But had my Dad asked me if I wanted to get rich, he might have grabbed my attention. If he'd told me that investing might be one of the best side hustles out there, I would have wanted to know more.

Are you interested in learning more?

While investing can be complicated & intimidating, it doesn't have to be. There are simple approaches to investing too. Investing can turn your few hard-earned dollars into something big. So long as you get started early enough to let time do its thing.
I want that for my kids.

While investing doesn't come with any guarantees, starting early might give a young investor a shot at growing some decent wealth. I hope this works. For them & for you. The more times you can double your money between right now & when you decide to get off the treadmill, the more you'll enjoy the freedom that follows.

Paul
March 17th, 2023

Using this Book

Just about everyone I know wants to be rich. But far fewer people take the time to learn about investing. If you want to grow your financial wealth, you need to invest in something. Some choose to invest in themselves, in property, or in their own business. Others choose to invest in the stock market. Most of us do a combination of some, or all, of those things. Regardless of your investment choices, you should know about the potential for investing some of your money in the stock market. Even if you choose to invest with an advisor, you should know enough to assess the quality & value of the advice you are paying for. This book provides an overview of the investing process. And its potential for growing wealth.

Each succeeding section of this book takes you up a notch on the investing ladder & expands the range of options open to you. Don't worry if you find yourself struggling a little as we climb the ladder. Even the simpler strategies have great potential. Hang in there, you'll see.

Part 1 covers the basics for getting started with index investing. Though the strategy here is simple, it has been an effective path to wealth for many investors. And it is an approach recommended by some of the most astute investors to have ever walked the earth.

There is one simple thing covered here that is essential for growing wealth. Do not ignore it!

In Part 2, we explore some of the challenges you will face along the way. If you don't understand the things that can undermine your wealth-building efforts, you will sacrifice some of the potential. Here we learn to tune out the noise & to appreciate the true power of time. When it comes to growing wealth, time is magical.

Part 3 broadens the approach. While the simple approach has been the most successful in the past, perhaps that won't hold true for the future. There are more diverse strategies recommended by leading economists & experts in the field. Today, there are simple solutions for these more sophisticated strategies too. And we'll look at some things best avoided.

While buying funds (baskets of stocks) might be the best approach for many, Part 4 looks at a stock picking strategy. This strategy is relatively easy to understand. And it's a good way to learn about the challenges of stock picking. It might get you thinking about retirement differently too. Especially if you're a fan of the FIRE movement & very early retirement is one of your goals.

Part 5 covers several areas of investment that fall outside the stock market. Many of the chapters here are on topics that thousands of books have been written about. While a short chapter cannot do justice to these topics, it's more about getting you to think about how some of these ideas fit together with a financial plan. And how a financial plan is a very important part of your overall plans for living a full life.

Part 6 ties up some loose ends & provides an idea or two for those who made it this far & don't know what to do next. It includes some additional encouragement to get started, so I might repeat one or two things here. You know Dads like to do that sometimes!

Ready to give it go?

Part 1 - Getting Started

The biggest advantage a young investor has is time. The younger you are, the greater the chances that you can grow your wealth. All you need do is save & invest while you are young. And add a little more to your portfolio from every paycheque. Sounds easy, eh?

Judging by how few people do it, it can't be. But if you can keep it simple, there's a better chance that you will succeed.

Is there a simple approach that works?

1. Investing Advice from Dad?

I started investing when I was a lot older than my kids are today & it was a disaster. Since I worked in the industry, I thought I knew the tech business well. I began investing in hot tech stocks leading up to the peak of the dot-com bubble in 2000. There were no trading apps back then, so I had to call my broker, on an ancient landline, to place a trade. Thanks to his advice, I had some money in companies like Microsoft (MSFT), Pfizer (PFE) & Bell Canada Enterprises (BCE), now BCE Inc. But my personal favourite was Nortel Networks Corporation (NT). This was *the* iconic Canadian tech giant back then. I was proud to be the owner of shares in a company that was putting Canada's tech sector on the world map. Nortel was going to make me rich.

Then the bubble burst.

After the first leg of the crash, I was trying to follow some guru's investing advice about holding good companies for the long haul. I was sticking with my stocks. As the market continued to tumble, I lost it. I was terrified & I screamed … Sell … Sell … Sell! Things were dropping so fast that even my broker couldn't talk me into staying in the market. Most were now losing positions, but I sold everything.

Except Nortel.

I was a believer in this great company. Surely it would bounce back. Had I held onto my shares of Microsoft, Pfizer & BCE, I would have done okay. They eventually recovered & went on to new highs over the decades since.

While my Nortel shares went to zero.

Nada, nothing, zilch!

A very hard lesson that. And one that scared me out of the market for too many years. After panic selling following a crash, sitting on the sidelines in cash for the years that followed proved to be another expensive lesson. Had I stayed invested, I would eventually have recovered my losses & more. A lot more.

Funny enough, & despite the losses, I still love my memories of the glory days of Nortel. And I still enjoy a morning coffee from my Nortel mug.

But falling in love with a hot stock is probably not the best approach to investing!

2. Crystal Ball Investing

I've admitted to only a couple of my past mistakes, but there have been others along the way. Fortunately, so far, none as costly as those in the last chapter. Fingers crossed, the worst is behind me. Though you can never say never when it comes to investing. Even when we make good decisions, the outcome might not be what we expect. Why?

Because nobody can predict what any market or stock will do going forward. Nobody. Even the experts can not predict the market movement consistently. They might know a lot of stuff, but they don't know if the stock they are recommending today will be up or down tomorrow. Despite the countless hours I've spent learning, I can not pick one single stock that comes with a guarantee of increasing in value. However, there are strategies & approaches that increase the probability of success over the long term. Nobody has a crystal ball. But going with a simpler strategy, one that increases the chances of winning, beats the crystal ball approach for most of us. Almost all the time.

While knowledge doesn't guarantee future success, it may help avoid some dumb mistakes. Avoiding disaster is a big part of the wealth-building process. Investing can be a minefield. Getting blown up destroys confidence & portfolio value. And the opportunity for building greater wealth over the long term.

Understanding what you are investing in, & why, is important. And it might not be as complex as you think.

There are some simple investing strategies that have proven successful over the course of time. Those are the strategies that we start out with here.

3. Why Invest Then?

Given the stories of my personal disasters with investing, you might not want to listen to anything I say. So let me share Warren Buffett's advice with you instead. Mr. Buffett is the chairman and CEO of Berkshire Hathaway. A conglomerate that has provided investors a return greater than that of the market over many decades. In his 2013 Letter to Shareholders, he advises individual **and** professional institutional investors to buy a low-cost, market index fund. In fact, he gives the same advice to the trustees of his estate. These are the lawyers who will manage his wife's inheritance. He asks that they allocate 90% to a very low-cost S&P 500 Index® fund. With the remaining 10% going to short-term, government bonds. In fact, he specifically says that it should be a Vanguard fund. Vanguard is the company founded by Jack Bogle, another of the world's legendary investors. His gift to retail investors, that's us, was the low-cost index fund. Sadly, he passed away in 2019. But the internet is filled with his words of wisdom. Take the time to listen to, & learn from, both these investing sages.

Starting out, & possibly all the way to retirement, it might be better for you to take the advice of Messrs. Buffett & Bogle over anything you read here or anywhere else.

Why?

Because "the market" has returned about 10% annually. It has done that for the past century or thereabouts. There are no guarantees that it will do the same over the course of your lifetime, of course. But if it does, & if you are invested in "the market", you'll likely have far fewer investing regrets than I have. A $50k investment in the market by age 30, with that 10% annual return compounding, would be worth almost $1.6 million by retirement day. In other words, if you get that $50k invested early enough in your life, you could become a millionaire without ever having to save another penny. The opportunity I missed makes me weep.

Just for fun, if you added an additional $100 a week to your $50k investment, from age 30 onwards, the portfolio could be worth almost $3.2 million by the time you retire. Of course, it's tough to come up with fifty grand to get started. But a 20-year-old, starting from zero, who saves & invests $100 a week might get close to $4.5 million by retirement day.

Isn't that just crazy? Totally unbelievable, eh? Compound growth is totally mind-boggling. But don't take my word for it, find a compound return or compound interest calculator online & see for yourself.

Along with some of the other great information at this site, I like the compound interest calculator at the Ontario Security Commission's website.
You can find it at ... www.getsmarteraboutmoney.ca
This calculator shows a great graphical representation of how little you need to save, to make such a lot. But *only* if you start young. And let it run for a long, long

time. Warren Buffett, a multi-billionaire, is not only smart but, at the age of 92, he's been doing this for a while now. Time is the real juice in this game. Get a compound growth or compound interest app for your phone. It's a great motivational tool. And you only need to stay motivated long enough to get things up & running.

If you get all pumped from using your compound growth calculator, you could start out by putting some money into Vanguard Canada's S&P 500 Index® ETF, ticker symbol VFV. An ETF is an Exchange Traded Fund. Exchange Traded Funds are baskets of stocks that trade on a stock exchange, under one ticker symbol, like VFV. This one is the Canadian-listed equivalent of the ETF recommended by Warren Buffett. It holds the same basket of US stocks. But VFV trades on the Toronto Stock Exchange & it's in Canadian dollars. We'll talk about investing through the American exchanges later, but for now, let's keep it simple & stick with Canadian-listed ETFs.

If you have spare contribution room (check at your CRA My Account & on your Notice of Assessment from last year's tax return) & spare cash, you might start by investing inside your Tax-Free Savings Account (TFSA). In addition to Vanguard's VFV ETF, you will find similar products from other financial companies. There are several funds tracking the S&P 500 Index®. This index is often considered to be representative of "the market", & it's made up of 500 of the largest American companies trading on the US stock market. This is a very simple & straightforward way to start. But I suggest you only do it with money that you won't need for a long time. Like 'til retirement day. You do not invest in the market if you'll need the money in the foreseeable future. While the long trend is up, it can be a bit of a roller-coaster ride along the way. That's the scary thing about investing.

We will go into the different accounts available later, along with some of the pros & cons of each. But if you think the TFSA is a savings account where you just store cash, you are going to love what investing might be able to do for you inside this tax-sheltered account.

4. Canada, eh!

Already I am deviating from Mr. Buffett's advice! My excuse is that he was speaking to American investors. I think you should have some Canadian content in your portfolio too. While Canada's stock market is only about 3% of the global market, there's nothing wrong with having some of your savings in an ETF filled with Canadian companies. And I don't mind being more biased to the Canadian side than our share of the global market would suggest. For the most part, we are an economically sound, resource rich, & politically stable democracy, with broad respect for the rule of law. That's not a bad environment to invest in. And, as you'll see, there are some other advantages for a Canadian to invest in Canadian companies.

Mr. Buffett has an unshakeable faith in America but occasionally other parts of the world, including Canada, can do better. An investment in the US market, via an S&P 500 Index® fund, in late 1999 would have shown about zero return after 10 years. During that same ten-year period, a Canadian fund tracking our S&P/TSX 60 Index® would have more than doubled. If you'd started investing in the US market back then, imagine how shaken your faith in Mr. Buffett's advice would be after ten years. Though the real lesson here is not that his advice was wrong. But that we need to be as patient as he is. That decade, dubbed the "Lost Decade" in the

American market, underperformed because the crippling dot-com crash in 2000 was followed by the American financial crisis of 2008. The first took out the tech sector, along with anything remotely connected to it. And the financial crash crushed the American financial & housing sectors. While there are no guarantees things will work the same way in the future, the Canadian banking & housing sectors held up well during that period of American uncertainty. Having something invested in the Canadian market would have made a lot of sense back then. Diversification across different markets can soften the blow when one market tanks & the other doesn't. Over time, however, the American market caught back up again. And it went on to outperform the Canadian market since. That is the nature of markets. And this illustrates the potential for diversification to provide a little extra protection for a portfolio.

The Canadian market is too small & too narrowly focused to go all in. Our market is heavily concentrated in financial, energy & materials companies. With very limited exposure to sectors like technology & healthcare. These are two of the big sectors in the US market. Along with geographic diversity, diversification across several industry sectors is also important. Despite Mr. Buffett's recommendation to go all in on America, I see nothing wrong with splitting an investment portfolio between the US & Canada.

There are several ETFs that track the Canadian market.

I'm going to use XIU, the Blackrock iShares® S&P/TSX 60 Index® ETF, for this exercise. This fund is the evolution of the world's first-ever, publicly traded ETF. It launched in 1990 & contains 60 of the biggest companies trading on the Canadian market. Though XIU has a higher MER than the American market ETF, currently 0.18% for XIU versus 0.09% for VFV, it performs well. The MER is the Management Expense Ratio, or the percentage fee deducted by the fund managers, for managing the fund. You don't pay extra on top of buying shares of the ETF, these fees are automatically removed inside the fund. We'll come back to fees in more detail later.

You can build an equity (that means stock) portfolio around Vanguard Canada's VFV, tracking the American market. With BlackRock's iShares® XIU for the Canadian portion. That is only two tickers to purchase, still very simple. VFV contains over 500 hundred of America's biggest publicly traded businesses. While XIU has 60 of Canada's largest companies. You can split the purchase in whatever ratio you want, it could be 70% US & 30% Canada to start. Some investors favour the Canadian market more heavily, others less. Whatever ratio you choose, the greater diversification obtained by investing in more than one market can be beneficial. There are no guarantees, of course, but if you create this two-fund portfolio & add to it regularly for the next 40 years or so, you might do okay.

But there's a little wealth-building secret you need to know to make it all happen.

5. The Secret to Building Wealth

This isn't really a secret but so many of us don't do it, it might as well be. One of **the** keys to growing your wealth is to have an **automated process** for saving & investing. Regularly. You set it, forget it, & then go check your portfolio about 30 or 40 years from now. I'm not kidding, that might be all you need to do. But you must **start** doing it.

Yes, you do need to save & invest enough to make it all work. And the earlier you start the better. But the key here is the "*automated process*" bit. Most of us are pretty awful at developing new habits. You can listen to motivational speakers 'til the cows come home, but most of the buzz is gone by Monday morning. A vision board for getting rich sounds like fun, but it's worthless if you are not saving & investing regularly. I'm sure you've already thought about how important saving & investing are. How's that going so far? Are you on the road to riches already?
But you're going to get round to it, right!

If you automate the process, you'll never have to think about forcing yourself to get round to it again. Set up an automatic transfer out of your regular bank account & into your brokerage account. Check your contribution room first & then move it into your TFSA. Do **not** overshoot your TFSA contribution limit, the CRA (Canada Revenue Agency, the tax man) will penalise you. But **do** set things up so that your savings are moved **out** of your regular "spending" account **automatically**. You should then buy more shares of your favourite, low-cost, index-tracking ETFs. Even if you don't invest it right away, & you should, the money will be safely out of the spending account. From which you're far more likely to suck it out & spend it. Match your transfer frequency to the frequency of your paycheque. Automatically move the money out after payday, each & every pay period. You can set this up online in minutes. Do it. And you'll never have to beat yourself up for not saving again. This is so simple. But so powerful. You need to get it done.

When it comes to saving & investing ...

Automation beats Motivation! Every time.

The whole "Get Rich Quick" thing is way overhyped online & in social media. The headlines say you can fast-track your way to mega-millions. It's mostly marketing messages that few can deliver on. The hype is from people trying to sell us something. It's about them getting rich, not us. It's exhausting & confusing reading this stuff. The path to wealth shouldn't begin with a feeling of confusion. Despite the ups & downs of the markets, growing wealth is a process of discipline & diligence. You can get there by the patient practice of doing small & simple things regularly.
Sounds almost Zen-like, doesn't it!

6. Setting Up a Brokerage Account

If you are tech-savvy & used to paying your bills electronically, you'll find it easy to learn an online brokerage interface. I suggest you do not trade on your phone. It's far too easy to panic sell on a phone. Or to buy something while you're partying on a beach during spring break. Starting out, get your experience by only investing while sitting comfortably at a big screen. Mistakes working with a brokerage account can be costly. There is less chance of doing the wrong thing when you are driving a big screen. Don't put that decimal point in the wrong place! If you are not tech savvy & you still want to invest without paying an advisor, you really have no choice. You'll have to learn how to use an online brokerage account.

All the big Canadian banks have brokerage arms & there are other online brokerages that are not affiliated with the banks. Some of the bank brokerages offer practice trading accounts. A couple of the other online brokerages have time-limited trials, so you can test drive the platform. None of the brokerages want to give you an unlimited, unfettered, practice account for free. Because they offer some useful tools & resources inside. These tools have value. Getting you to sign up for an account is the price you pay for access to them. If you're already doing your regular banking with one of these institutions, you might be eligible to use that bank's practice account. Ask.

When choosing a brokerage, the fees charged will be a big part of your decision. Fees will have an impact on your returns wherever they occur. Given enough time, even small fees can have a very big impact on your portfolio. Compare things like account carrying fees or administration charges, trading commission costs, foreign exchange fees &, in case you change your mind later, account closure & transfer fees. Wealthsimple Trade offers free accounts & free trading. Though it has some differences to the typical big bank brokerages, it's a popular choice for new investors. National Bank of Canada announced free trading of stocks & ETFs on their brokerage platform in 2021. Other banks paid attention. Most of the big bank brokerages now have a range of ETFs that you can buy commission-free. You may already be banking with one of these banks. There is often an account administration fee for a TFSA account. For most of the banks, that gets waived while you are under a certain age. Or if you have more than a certain number of dollars or investments in the account. Each bank has a slightly different account fee structure & different fee waiver conditions. Check with your own bank. These fees matter. All fees matter. They erode your returns.

If you start out small & you need to invest often, trading commissions can hurt a lot. You don't want to get stuck investing $100 a week with a trading fee of $9.95. After paying that commission, a $100 trade needs to grow by 11.1% just to get you back to even. That's more than a year of the market's average annual return. Trading fees on small trades are too big a hit to take. Starting out, if you can only save & trade with small amounts, the less you need to pay for each trade. Preferably zero. Do you know that trading costs of **only** $10 a week will cost you about **four hundred & fifty thousand dollars** in lost opportunity cost from age 20 to 65. Money spent on fees could have been invested. I'm not kidding here, use your compound growth app & prove it to yourself. Start with a $10 investment & add $10 a week over 45 years at a 10% growth rate. Time does funny things with money, but it compounds in both directions. Up for investments, down for the opportunity lost when money goes to costs.

Time giveth but fees taketh away!

It this is all new to you, the following italicised paragraphs will terrorise you. But don't let them paralyse you. I'll fix it at the end of the chapter!

WARNING!

*Once you set up an account, do **not** randomly move money in & out of registered accounts. There are rules about what you can & can't do with registered accounts. Day trading is considered a business, even in a TFSA, & the proceeds are taxable. There may be tax penalties & consequences if you do the wrong thing with any account, registered or not. You do not cash out of one brokerage account, take the money out, & move it to another. You, personally, can not transfer TFSA money to another brokerage under the tax shelter, that must be done between the new & existing brokerage. You must ask the brokerage to do it. Take money out of an RRSP & you'll be taxed on it as income & you lose the* *contribution room, permanently. Again, the brokerage must move it for you. There are CRA approved ways of doing all these things, while maintaining the tax sheltering properties of the account. Go to the CRA site & learn about the limitations & complications. Don't screw up with registered investing accounts. Until you learn enough to play safely, check with the CRA, your bank, your brokerage, or a professional advisor before messing with moving your money. Don't mess up when moving money or holdings in & out of, or between, registered accounts or different brokerages. Make sure you follow the official rules & instructions.*

Okay, I apologise for all that fearmongering, but it is important to know in case you change your mind after opening your first account. Or in case you decide to switch accounts because of something you read on social media. Social media is not a recommended source of decision-making information. You can get good info there, but there's a lot of nonsense online too. Registered accounts are not like regular bank accounts, so don't do all that swapping & changing stuff. Starting out, take it slow & easy. You should just be buying & holding anyway.

There are some advantages to having everything under one roof starting out. Despite the potential fee & cost implications, sticking with your own bank's brokerage can be a great way to start. Moving savings into a brokerage account, for example, can feel more comfortable for a beginner when everything is under the roof of their regular bank. It's familiar & you can even drop into your local branch to ask questions of a real person. Of course, you still need to check the fees & conditions surrounding opening & running an account there. And on how to minimise those. If you can have the account fees waived & if you can buy the major market index ETFs commission-free, that could work well. No trading commission on ETFs is one of the most important considerations for a beginning investor who will be investing small amounts frequently. Get that done & you're locked & loaded.

So you're all fired up now, but you have a lousy job. It doesn't pay much & you really don't have much to save.

What can you do?

7. Investing on Minimum Wage

It's easy to talk about investing for big returns if you have a big salary. But what if you're on minimum wage? The size of the paycheque doesn't change the rules of the game. But the less money you make, the more critical it is that you start sooner. Let's be real here, we would all rather have the bigger paycheque. But you'll find some well-paid people hitting retirement in poor financial shape too. A kid finishing high school starts working years ahead of someone who commits to a primary degree, a masters, & a doctorate. Imagine our high school graduate living at home for those same years that the university student is borrowing money to pay for an education. Investing some of the savings that come with doing that, it is possible for that kid to retire with a bigger portfolio than the university graduate.

Am I dreaming here?

Okay, let's look at it this way then …

The average minimum wage across Canada's provinces & territories, at the end of 2022, is about $14.36 per hour. Starting at age 20, saving & investing the equivalent of one hour's work a week could turn into more than six hundred thousand dollars by retirement day. Save two hours wages every week & that's over $1.2 million. Wild, eh!?!

Yes, I know it's tough to save on minimum wage. But a kid who can save & invest even a little, but regularly & consistently, all the way to age 65, can look forward to a more comfortable retirement than many. Can you save the equivalent of one hour's work a week to grow your wealth? Imagine what it would be like if you saved more than one or two hours wages a week from an early age. Invest a few hours of your earnings every week & time will take care of growing your wealth. What if you also invested your bonus money, your raises, or your tips?

I want to keep talking here, to encourage you to get started, but a picture is worth more than six hundred thousand words. And dollars!

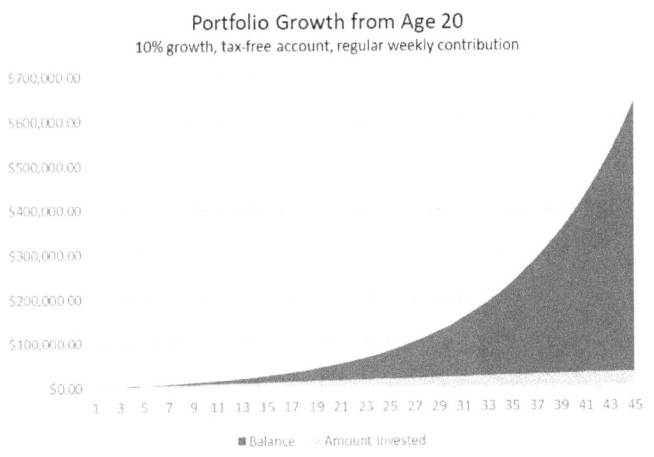

Fig 1.7.1 Investing One Hour's Work a Week on Minimum Wage

A twenty-year-old has 45 years between turning twenty & retirement at 65. I know that seems like forever. But it'll pass regardless of how long you feel it'll take. Why not save & invest a little to help pass the time. Let your little portfolio do its thing in the background. It might surprise you down the road. Look at the little light-coloured sliver at the bottom of the chart. It shows how little was saved & invested to make so much. The dark coloured part of the chart shows the investment returns on that small sliver of savings. Small sums of money, invested regularly, for a long enough time, can produce magical results. Things won't be as perfectly clean & smooth as this chart shows. There will be bumps & potholes along the way. But this approach might be the best shot most of us have at building some wealth from scratch.

If your earnings expectations are low in your current day job, start young & aim high with your savings rate. Invest those savings regularly & your wealth-building story might have a happy ending.

8. Starting Out

Setting up an automatic savings process to fund your investments is key. Most of us don't do it. No matter the size of your paycheque, or how little your savings, doing this will make a difference for you. Keep it simple, have a process, & then automate that process. For anything you can't put on autopilot, do the same thing, at the same time, after every pay cheque. Make it a habit, a regular routine. That way, you won't have to think about what to do every time. If you need to think about doing it every week, or every month, you'll deliberate, you'll procrastinate, you'll skip one every now & then, & you'll eventually abandon the process. Automate & habituate the process instead. Then treat the investment in your TFSA like it's locked in 'til retirement.

Because it probably should be. You're on your way!

Is that all there is to it? No, not quite. Buckle up!

Part 2 - Wealth Building Challenges

At this point, I know you're thinking I've made this whole investing thing sound far too simple. And you are right, I did make it sound simple. Deliberately so. Because I hope that helps you get started. The benefit of starting early is the one thing that nobody argues against.

In Part 2, we are going complicate things a little.

1. Is it Really That Easy?

The investing strategy we looked at is so simple that I'm sure you have questions. Like can it really be that simple? Yes, it can. But even when saving & investing is that simple, it is never easy. It's still risky. It can be scary. There are challenges along the way. We need to figure out how to handle things when the market crashes. What should we do in a recession? And though this might be a little ways down the road for you, should the approach change as your portfolio grows?

As you learn more about investing, you will be bombarded by a million conflicting streams of advice. Do this. Don't do that. Globally diversify. Stocks are better than ETFs. Small cap stocks are better than large cap. Buy growth stocks. You must have bonds. Crypto is the new millionaire-maker. You need a professional advisor. And who knows what else. Everyone has an opinion these days. We can all be influenced by someone telling a good story. And there are a lot of good story tellers out there. Start out with a simple approach & be wary of anyone who tells you it needs to be complicated. That what you are doing isn't sophisticated enough. That it's not the best way to grow your wealth. As soon as you feel the urge to deviate from a simple index investing strategy, learn more before you do. And question everything as you learn. The first question should be: how does what they recommend compare to Mr. Buffett's advice?

We are going to look at & compare other strategies, including buying individual stocks, so you'll be better prepared for those conversations. You may even choose to use one of the other strategies. But no matter the approach you choose to take, try to keep it simple. And always work within the limits of your current level of knowledge. Unfortunately, for all of us, it will always be true that we don't know what we don't know. It's when we think we know stuff that investing can get dangerous. And, even for those highly educated professionals, things don't always go as planned.

Regardless of how far beyond the starter ETF portfolio strategy you choose to go, you will need your own process. One that helps make it easy for you to decide on the purchase & sale of investments on a regular basis. The simpler & more repeatable that process is, the better. If you don't understand what you are doing & why you are doing it, then don't do it yet. Learn more first. There may be times in your life when you will be just too busy to pay attention to investing. That's when a well thought out strategy & process help most. Knowing in advance what you should buy & being focused on your process can be a good thing during turbulent markets too. As you learn & as you are exposed to conflicting opinions, things can get complicated. It gets even more interesting when the markets don't behave as we want them to.

2. Know the Score

How much will you need to feel financially free?

That's the million-dollar question. Or maybe it's the two-, or three-million-dollar question for you. That number depends on *your* plans for retirement. The numbers thrown about online suggest that retirees today will need somewhere between $700k & $1.4m for a comfortable retirement. The little "k" means thousand & the "m" million. Many Canadians facing retirement don't have that much. You can spend time on the Statistics Canada website if you want to frighten yourself into saving. While about 30% of Canadians are debt-free & have savings, another 30% have next to nothing saved for retirement. Going into retirement, we have no choice but to make do with whatever we have.

Saving & investing is not about making do. It's about starting early enough to make a difference down the road. If you qualify for full Canada Pension Plan (CPP) & Old Age Security (OAS), & most Canadians don't, that's only a foundation for retirement income. People with an employer sponsored pension scheme generally retire wealthier than those who do not have a pension plan with their job. Work pensions get a good result because employers *automate* the saving & investing program for their employees. Generally, homeowners have a far greater net worth than renters. Taking on a mortgage is a self-imposed, but *automated*, saving & investing plan.

If you are renting, it is even more critical that you start saving & investing early. More renters retire poor. We will come back to the value & challenges of home ownership again. But the bottom line is that all these early choices, like getting a job with a pension or deciding to buy a home, can have a huge impact later in life. And you'll notice that these wealth builders are all about having an automated process. One that works over a long, long time. Automation can save us from our own lack of discipline & our very human inclination to do nothing to prepare for a retirement that's way too far in the future to be considered urgent today.

If you are lucky enough to retire with a defined benefit pension, that can take away a lot of the stress. Defined benefit pensions pay you for the rest of your life. These pensions are often index linked, so that your income increases in line with the consumer price index or inflation. In other words, as costs increase so does your pension. Very neat. DB pensions mostly come with a government job these days. Private sector pensions, from those companies that offer them to their employees, tend to be the defined contribution type nowadays. You pay something into the pension plan & the employer matches some or all of your contributions. That's a great way to go too, it's like free money from your employer. With a defined contribution pension plan, however, there is no income guarantee in retirement. And you are at the mercy of the performance of whatever investments the pension plan puts your money into. But whether it's Defined Benefit or Defined Contribution, it's still great if your job comes with a pension plan. If signing up is optional, make sure you do. And contribute enough to get the maximum amount from the employer match. You can double your money right away with the employer contribution. You can't get that kind of instant return from the market.

Why am I drivelling on about all this pension stuff? Because if you don't have a job with a pension plan, personal retirement savings are really, truly, incredibly essential. You'll have nothing else. Even if you have a company pension plan, you should save & invest more anyway. You never know when you'll be forced to change jobs or get fired & your pension plan contributions stop! Each person's needs & wants will be different. But starting your process early & doing it consistently is never wrong.

A phrase you'll often hear in the financial services industry is that past performance does not guarantee future results. What if the market doesn't deliver that 10% return over the course of your investing lifetime? While there is nothing wrong with hoping for a great outcome, being real, you need to plan for a worse one. Use a compound growth calculator to figure out what your retirement might look like if the market delivers lower returns than its historical returns. Or if you choose a more conservative approach to investing, rather than investing everything in the stock market.

See what the numbers look like with an 8% return. Perhaps it will only be 5% with your investment choices. Could it be worse than that? I don't know. But it's your life we're talking about here, you must live it your way. But do look at worst case scenarios & plan accordingly.

The other challenge is that the annualised 10% returns of the market are not delivered smoothly. You will have some huge market downturns along the way. Long-term saving & investing **should** produce the desired result. But what if it doesn't work that way for you? You certainly won't feel great if a portfolio you've spent decades building gets cut in half one Monday morning. There's no way I know of mentally preparing for this ahead of time. But it will happen. Try to steel yourself for when the big crash strikes. Okay, you can freak out. But keep on keeping on anyway. Keep on saving & investing regularly. **Especially** through the crashes & the downturns. Try to think of it like your favourite ETFs just went on sale. Because, during a crash, that is what is happening. Though we'll consider other ways to mitigate these downturns, surviving & investing through periods of volatility is the only way to build up tolerance for it. It's not easy. But that's the reality.

Ah, what am I talking about … nobody can tolerate huge drops in the value of their portfolio. Feel free to throw up. But sticking with the plan & the process usually produces the best results over time.

Investing can be tough, eh!

3. Wealth Building in a Nutshell

A lot of what we need to understand about growing wealth through investing goes something like this ...

1   Beating the Market ... is the holy grail for investors. The reality is that, after fees, most professional investors don't beat the market, most of the time. Yet, somehow, most of us amateur investors think we can. And, year after year, millions of us go on to prove we can't. Forget about beating the market, just try to keep pace with it. This is not a bad thing. Just keeping pace with the market has tremendous wealth building potential.

2   Paying for Advice ... the financial services industry is interesting; in that you sometimes don't get what you think you are paying for. You might think you are paying for improved returns but, after fees, most advisors & fund managers cannot beat the average market return over time. Despite that, you can pay a lot for advice. High fees can be a huge destroyer of wealth.

3   Debt is Deadly ... if you don't realise this early enough you will, short of getting very lucky, probably retire poor. Expensive debt is a total wealth killer. You can't invest if every penny of your paycheque is servicing debt. Avoid debt, especially expensive debt, like the plague.

4   The Path to Wealth ... for most people is paved by saving & investing small amounts regularly. Make this your mission. Then automate the process so

you can't screw it up. Save little & often, invest inexpensively, & you might have a shot at building wealth.

5   The Magic Ingredient … is time. It is almost impossible for the human brain to grasp this well enough, & emotionally enough, to get really excited about it. But time is the magic ingredient. Today, you think you have lots of time & too little money. Wrong! That is the ***exactly the opposite*** of what you need to be thinking in order to build wealth. Given enough time, a little money can be worth a lot down the road.

The following chapters will give you a little more insight on why these wealth-building commandments fly so far under the radar for so many.

4. Beating the Market

I like to think I'm smarter than average. In fact, despite carrying a few extra pounds, I might even be better-looking than average. And while I can't run very fast anymore, I compensate by believing that I'm a better driver than average. I bet you think great things of yourself too. And that's good. We should feel good about ourselves. But this very human need to feel good about ourselves can be dangerous when it comes to investing. It sometimes makes us think that we're smarter than the market.

As you learn more, you might start thinking that you are smart enough to outsmart the market. I've been there. I thought I could look at stock charts & intuit something that no one else on the planet could. I couldn't. The chances of you doing that are very unlikely too. Professional investors are trying to beat the average market returns year in & year out. They have the best education, premium equipment, the latest software & algorithms, & they do this for a living, every trading day. Most of them do not beat the market, most of the time. That might sound crazy, but it's true. There are those very rare few who have stood the test of time. But most active investment managers cannot beat the market over the long haul. Especially when you deduct the cost of the fees they charge for trying. The numbers vary from about 50% to almost 100% of actively managed funds underperforming their benchmark index. The longer the time span considered, the fewer that can keep up. And if you find a winning fund or portfolio from last year, the chances are pretty high that it will not perform as well next year. In other words, by the time you find out a fund manager did well, you are probably already too late to join that party. If you think it's tough to pick the winning stocks, it might be even tougher to pick a winning fund manager. Or a winning financial advisor. Most fund managers & advisors, after fees, provide below average returns compared to the indices they compare themselves against. The S&P Dow Jones Indices Group publishes their SPIVA® scorecard every 6 months. This compares the performance of actively managed funds against the indices, by country or region. SPIVA® means S&P Indices Versus Active. You won't believe how poor the results are for active management. Go check it out.

What does all this mean for a DIY investor?

Most of us cannot build a portfolio of stocks that will outperform the market either. Being real, if the full-time pros can't do it, there is no way we're doing it. Look, I'm not saying that you're not the special one. The ultimate stock picker. Maybe you are the next great smart one. But I suggest start your investing journey with a little humility. It's tough to beat the market. On the other hand, average market returns might be enough.

Investing might be the only field where average performance puts you in the top performance tier!

5. Paying for Advice

If we have a toothache, we pay the dentist to fix it. If a bottle of goopy stuff doesn't clear a clogged drain, we're happy to pay the plumber to do it for us. If we have a problem with our finances, shouldn't we just pay a professional for financial advice?

Probably, eh? Maybe.

We pay for stuff because we need it. Or because we want it. Advice can fall into either of, or both, those categories. An investor who just can't get comfortable going it alone will need some handholding. Other investors, unwilling to put in the time to learn & understand, may choose to pay for advice. For them, that is the wise choice. Going it alone requires learning & work. And the ability to weather the financial storms. Alone. But figuring out how much to pay for advice & what that advice is worth takes work too. You need to put in the time because a potentially significant portion of a DIY investor's returns can come from the fees saved. When it comes to financial advice, annual fees are an ongoing & enduring cost that can really eat into long term returns. Fees really matter.

There is no free lunch when it comes to financial advice. Free financial advice usually comes with higher product fees. Visit your local financial institution for free advice & you will likely be offered the company's own mutual funds. Canadian mutual fund fees can be very expensive, many of them charge over 2% annually.

Whip out your compound growth calculator & you'll find that $50k turns into about $1.6 million over 35 years, with a 10% rate of return. But if your return drops from 10% to 8% because of fees, the portfolio only grows to about 800k over that same time. That 2% reduction in the return rate eliminates about $800k of your total return potential. About **half** your portfolio potential will be consumed by that **small** fee. Fees matter. Always check the long-term impact of fees with a compound growth calculator. Our heads don't do compound growth math very well.

The advisory space in Canada is a bit of an unregulated mess. There are so many licences & certifications, it's hard to tell who does what. And what their responsibilities towards you, the client, are. Outside financial institutions that offer free advice, you'll find advisors that can manage a portfolio for a percentage fee of that portfolio. That can run around 1% annually, whether your portfolio goes up or down. Starting out, your portfolio will be too small to be of interest to many of the advisors that provide such services. There are advisors & financial planners that offer their services at an hourly rate. Or they can offer a package fee for a single service, like putting a financial plan together. Though these providers can offer great value, if you're just starting out, it can be difficult to justify the expenditure. Despite the costs, one of the standout advantages of working with an advisor is that they may save you from yourself. The problem with going it alone is just that: you are alone. Alone & fearful, DIY investors often panic & sell at the lows. Afraid that they are missing out, they may buy the current hot stock or sector as it approaches its peak. Buying high & selling low is not a recipe for success. You won't know how fearful & reactive you are going to be 'til you have been through a few downturns. And some booming upswings. An advisor who can calm you down & keep you on track during times of stress can quickly cover the cost of their fees. Even if their recommended portfolio is not beating the market.

If you have doubts on which path to follow, you can test drive it both ways. You could, for example, split your portfolio between an advisor-managed portfolio & a self-directed account. There can be advantages with this dual-pronged approach. You can use the lessons you learn from your advisor to set up your self-directed portfolio. Look up the story behind Robert Kirby's 'Coffee Can Portfolio' for the ultimate example of that. The wife paid for professional advice &, on the side, the husband bought the same stocks in his portfolio. Interestingly, the husband never sold anything when the advisor sold the wife's holdings. But his portfolio did better! It's a great story, you'll love it.

Robo-advisors are a more recent development in the industry & this might work for an investor who would prefer to have some professional guidance, but at a lower cost. Fees are around 0.5%, plus or minus, on top of the EFT fees. Usually, you answer a bunch of online questions to determine your investor profile, risk tolerance, & so on. The algorithms (no cute AI robot animation chatting with you online yet!) work out what your investment mix should be. Then the robo-advisor invests the money for you, in an asset mix appropriate for your investor profile. It will then rebalance the portfolio, as markets & allocations change. Some robo-advisory services offer email & phone access to human advisors too. This way, you might still feel like you have a real person in your corner. You have someone to call before you sell in a panic! These robo-advisory services are a great development in the industry & a great approach for a beginning investor who just can't get started on their own.

At the end of the day, the crux of the challenge for all investment advisors & fund managers is this: after ongoing portfolio management fees, most of them cannot beat the market over the long haul. Yet, outside of robo-advisors, few of them recommend just trying to track the market returns with a simple portfolio of low-cost index funds. Going it alone, a DIY investor who can learn to ride the market roller-coaster has the potential to get a result close to market returns. By simply buying low-cost index funds on a regular basis. With ETFs, you are still paying a small fee for someone to manage the index tracking on your behalf. You just can't call them up for a chat & to ask how the index is doing this week. Handholding is not included.

You'll need to learn some stuff before you can pick a good advisor. And by the time you know enough to pick a good advisor, you might know enough to test-drive going it alone.

6. Debt is Deadly

You can't save if you are up to your neck in debt. If you have a mountain of credit card debt that you are paying exorbitant interest rates on, you are toast. That's an emergency situation. Clear your credit card balance first. If you continue to use a credit card, clear the balance every month before its due date. The market return for the past century has been around 10% annually. What's the point in investing for a 10% return if you are blowing money on accumulating debt that costs twice that? The math is not complex here. Debt costing you 20% is a wealth killer. Check the Annual Percentage Rate (APR) in the small print of your credit card statement to see what your credit card debt is costing you. If you are servicing high interest debt with money that you could have saved & invested, you can't win this game. The market returns won't be smooth over short periods of time. But high interest debt is a wealth killer *all* the time. You should only invest when you expect the investment returns to be greater than the interest rate on your debt.

Dump the debt first.

And never get yourself into that position again.

Never.

This is so important; I feel an overwhelming urge to just go on & on about it. But there is nothing else to be said. Just read this page again. Twice.

If you are not up to your neck in debt already, you're ahead of many. Nearing the end of 2022, the average Canadian had $1.83 of debt for every $1 they earn. Don't be the average Canadian! Avoid debt like the plague. If you are mired in a swamp of debt, get out of it. Is there any debt that's good? We'll talk about that later.

Don't think I am against using credit cards, quite the opposite. Using a credit card can help you build your credit score. Depending on the features of the card, you can collect points, get cash back, or get insurance coverage on new purchases or car rentals. These all add value. But **only** if you clear the full balance when the bill is due. Every month. Some of us are wired to do this well. If you are not wired that way, keep your credit card in a block of ice.

There is a lot of information available on how to escape a debt spiral. Use it if you need it. But you already know what to do here. You need to allocate some money from **every** paycheque towards reducing debt. Automate this process too. Transfer debt servicing money out of your spending account after every pay day. Don't spend more than is left in that account between one paycheque & the next. And, above all, do not add any more debt. It's painful, but it's not rocket science.

Yes, I know life is tough. Some circumstances are impossible. You may feel you don't have choices or options. Feel whatever you will. But try tackling the problem anyway. Dedicate some number of hours of income towards debt reduction. Automate it out of your spending account. This should be your mission 'til you are debt-free. Then you can start dreaming of being rich.

Credit card debt is an easy one, the rates are ridiculous. What if you have a mortgage? Should you use a bonus cheque or an inheritance to invest or to pay down the mortgage? That's a tougher question to answer. Given the average market returns of 10% against a mortgage interest rate of 5%, the answer looks obvious, eh?

It's not.

Imagine investing a $100k inheritance in the market & then the market crashes. It takes years for the market to recover. Right after that disaster, inflation takes off & your mortgage comes up for renewal at a far higher interest rate. Soon as you sign up for the new, higher-rate mortgage, you lose your job. Now you might wish you'd paid down the mortgage instead. And that you'd bought that cheaper house!

Look, life is messy & unpredictable. Any combination of things can land you on your back. A simple comparison of debt interest rates to average market rates of return is not good enough to base these decisions on. Always be aware of potentially worse outcomes. And try to avoid them. Too much debt, regardless of interest rates & market returns, can wipe you out. That's not a good outcome.

Play defensively when it comes to assessing debt.

7. The Path to Wealth

It is almost impossible to get excited about saving little amounts regularly. Apps, online shopping, streaming services, & home delivery have conditioned us for instant gratification. We can feel the immediate joy of getting our hands on that new phone, jumping into the seat of a new car, going on vacation, or whatever. Online shopping can drop stuff off at our front door the same day now. It's all so insanely instant & gratifying. But taking a little slice off our paycheque every week for really long-term savings? Blah, how boring!

There really isn't much fun to saving a few bucks that won't show any significant return for yonks. And when it finally does, you're too old to enjoy it, right? No, that's not how it is. You'll just have to trust me on this one, there is no age limit on wanting to have fun.

Regularly saving & investing small amounts is about as exciting as watching paint dry. Until there is a market crash! Hey, I didn't promise that this investing thing would be all sunshine, sandy beaches, & little umbrella drinks. At least not 'til later. But saving & investing is a big deal. It's all about financial freedom. Whatever challenges come our way will come our way, whether we're rich or poor. While not all challenges can be taken care of by money, some can. And the feelings of relief & joy that come with financial freedom are wonderful. Imagine having enough money that you no longer *have* to carry on working. Even dreaming of that is exhilarating. Sure, it'll take a few years. But financial freedom is a great goal to shoot for. It's hard to make process & patience feel exciting. Automating the process is the best way to save us from our inability to create enough enthusiasm for it. And from our desire to spend everything on instantly gratifying our whims.

Despite how excruciatingly boring it all sounds, there really is excitement in all this. You'll see.

8. The Magic Ingredient

The magic ingredient is time. This concept is so important. If you save & invest 100 bucks a week, from age 20 to 65, you might have about $4.5 million in your account when you retire. Put it off to age 30 & that same hundred bucks a week grows to a little more than $1.6 million. Ignore things 'til you're 40 & you'll still have more than $0.5 million. Half a million isn't too shabby either. But you did notice how big an impact starting early has, right? All this dreaming assumes the historical 10% market returns & that everything is in a tax-sheltered account.

But wait ... we can still spend all our money on fun now & then can catch up later, eh? Like when we're earning the big bucks, right?

Go back & read that first paragraph again!

If you wait 'til age 40, you'd have to invest almost $800 *every week* to catch up to that twenty-year-old who only needed to sock away $100 a week. I know you're hoping you'll be earning more by then but that's eight times *more* in savings, *every week*, than if you'd started at age 20. At one hundred bucks a week, the twenty-year-old would have to save a total of about $230k to hit the $4.5m jackpot. The forty-year-old would have to save *over a million dollars* to get the same result. Saving sooner, earlier, younger means that you can get away with saving *way less* money to reach the same goal. If you think saving a hundred bucks a week is tough in your twenties, it might be lot tougher to save $800 a week at age 40. A stage of life when you might be paying for a mortgage, car loans, & kids. Even with a great job, saving $800 a week is a ridiculously tall order for most of us. Don't leave it late & have to play catch-up. I'm not saying it's impossible. But the vagaries of life can really screw up plans to play catch-up later.

Time is **the magic ingredient** in the recipe for growing wealth. The more time you have, the less you need to save. No matter when you start, once you start, time will start working for you. Unfortunately, there is one downside. It does take a long time. And the juice of compounding returns comes on far more strongly towards the end. To get the most out of it, you need to start early. You need to become a believer early. You need to act early. Adding a note about saving & investing to your to-do list just won't cut it.

Time is magic, but it drips away with each passing day. Don't waste it. If you've already left your twenties, your thirties, or any other decade, in the rear-view mirror, should you not even bother? Is it too late already? I think you know the answer to that question. An older investor may need to save more. Maybe invest more conservatively. And there will be fewer doubles before retirement day. But, regardless of age, doing nothing with the time remaining will likely not improve your chances for a more comfortable retirement.

Don't worry, you are not alone. I have regrets too!

9. The Wealth Building Mission

Let's just recap the key drivers of wealth building before we move on to looking at other challenges that will come up as your portfolio grows.

Forget about beating the market, just go for average market returns. This is one of the few opportunities in life where being average is a good thing. People following this strategy for 20, 30, or more, years are more likely be in the top tier for investment returns.

Financial advice comes with a cost. Assess the value of the advice relative to the cost. Today, those index-tracking ETFs we talked about come with an expense ratio of 0.09% for the US index & 0.18% for the Canadian index. The value of handholding aside, don't pay too much more for advice that delivers less.

Debt comes with the biggest cost of all. It takes your money & it prevents you from saving & investing. Don't do debt. Don't do debt. No, the repeat is not a typo. And please, don't do expensive debt!

Saving & investing small amounts regularly doesn't sound very exciting but if you automate the process, you are on the path. Automation beats motivation. Save & invest first. Cover your bills & obligations. Then squander the rest however you please.

You cannot get a daily motivational pump from the

whole magic-of-time thing. Time moves way too slowly to cater to our love of instant gratification. Best you can do is add a compound growth app to your phone. Run the numbers every now & then to get buzzed about your plan. And any time you want to blow cash on a new toy, plug in the numbers & see what the lost opportunity cost is by the time you'll retire.

Part 3 - The Sophisticated Investor

If you get really interested in investing, you will want to learn more. And as you explore, you will come across economists & experts who use strategies that offer opportunities to improve returns, that can protect your portfolio from downturns, or that provide some other positive outcomes. In Part 3, we will look at some of these strategies.

Let's complicate things a little!

1. ETF Investing

So far, we've only considered a couple of North American index ETFs for the starter portfolio. That & some cash in a high interest savings account might be as sophisticated as some will want to get starting out. But there are a lot more options out there. It feels like the number of ETFs available are catching up to the number of stocks that trade on the Canadian exchange now. As you learn more, you will probably be tempted to add some new dimension or strategy tweaks to your portfolio. In preparation for that, it can help to know a little more about what's on offer.

We can broadly divide funds into two major types: those that are actively managed & those that passively track an index. Within each of those categories, there are multiple variations & themes. Just because a fund is an "index" fund doesn't mean it's an automatic shoo-in for your portfolio. Index providers make money by creating & licensing indices. They will happily create an index for just about anything. And fund managers will create a fund for any index they think will attract investors & generate fees.

Passive index investing is usually the lowest fee approach & it's the approach that all the active strategies are trying to beat. You might even find some actively managed funds out there that do better than Warren Buffett's recommendation. But if you do come across one, don't be too surprised if you find it underperforms after you buy it. Low-cost, market-index investing is the way to go for most new investors. Maybe for most experienced investors too. We just need to figure out which market indices to follow.

Passive index funds aren't totally static. Index fund holdings change as the index managers play with the index constituents. They toss out stocks that no longer meet the rules of the index & bring in new ones that do. But trading activity inside index funds is usually far lower than in active funds. There are Trading Expense Ratio costs (TER) associated with ETFs. Those don't show up on the front page for the fund, they are often only reported in the downloadable documents. These TER costs are usually higher for actively managed funds. Because they do more trading. Interestingly, there are a couple of studies out there that suggest even the passive indices can be beaten. By being even more passive than the index. There is a paper entitled "The Long-term Returns on the Original S&P 500® Firms" by Siegel & Schwartz that you can find online. This paper shows that just holding the original components of the 1957 index, including the spinoffs & descendants of the original constituents, outperformed the regularly updated index since that time. There's another thing floating around the internet about a study supposedly done by a major financial institution that claimed the most successful retail portfolios belonged to dead people & investors who forgot they had a portfolio there. The message here is that you just buy a basket of good stocks & hold them. Forever. I know that approach would have worked for me. Had I held onto all my stocks after the dot-com crash, even with Nortel going to zero, I would be far ahead of where I find myself today. I might even have beaten the market!

Once you move away from passively managed ETFs, the fees go up. It's easy to find funds with fees of 0.5% in Canada. Some charge as much as 1% & more annually. Many mutual funds have fees in excess of 2%. Rather than just track an index, active fund management attempts to beat some benchmark or other. They may target making money in specific sectors. There are oil ETFs for when we think oil is going to run out & we'll all have to line up at the gas station. Gold ETFs are there for when we think the world as we know it is going to end. Tech ETFs because, when everyone is wildly optimistic, they seem have limitless upside potential. Then there are funds that do things many DIY investors find difficult to do. Some ETFs apply covered calls, leverage (borrowing money to invest in more stocks), & all kinds of financial shenanigans to try to wrest more gain or income out of an investment. This kind of active management requires more resource & that translates to higher fund fees. Higher fees work well for the company managing the fund. It's just difficult for them to beat a passive index fund by as much as the fees they charge. Buy actively managed ETFs with your eyes open. Perhaps not always but for many of these funds, you are likely to pay more & get less.

Despite the confusion created by the many ETFs on the market today, simple market index investing is a solid strategy for the DIY investor. If there is a low-cost ETF that aligns closely with your investing strategy, don't be embarrassed to invest in it. Sophisticated investing is understanding that it's all about patiently making more over the course of an investing lifetime. It's not about bragging rights on whose hot stock is leading the ticker tape parade this week.

But is our simple index investing strategy sophisticated enough?

Diversification is heavily promoted as a positive thing for investors, so you might find yourself wondering if being all in on the US & Canada is good enough.

But before we look at that, let's take a quick look at mutual funds.

2. ETFs or Mutual Funds?

Many years ago, I was sold some mutual funds. I paid extra to buy them. They performed poorly. And then I had to pay to get out of them. I have looked unkindly on mutual funds ever since. Read what follows with caution, as I might be a little biased here!

Canadian investors have a long-standing love affair going on with mutual funds. In bygone days, if you didn't buy stocks & bonds directly through a human broker, they were just about the only game in town. Buying stocks & bonds was way more difficult before the advent of the internet & online trading, so no surprise that. The mutual fund companies had a lock on the investment game & could charge high fees. Salespeople loved them because they received very nice commissions from selling mutual funds to their customers. While there have been some regulatory improvements, things haven't changed all that much today.

If you decide to check out the pros & cons of mutual funds versus ETFs online, be wary. There is some outdated information out there about the differences. One of the simplifications is that mutual funds are actively managed, while ETFs are passive. That might have been true when ETFs were in their infancy, but that is no longer the case today. This pitch goes hand in hand with the marketing spin that actively managed mutual funds offer the potential to beat the passive index ETFs, due to the great active management skills they employ. They have the potential, sure, but it doesn't happen often. And it's far less likely after fees are taken into account.

There are passively managed mutual funds that track the S&P500® index too. I just did a quick online search & three examples that came up on the first page of results had fees of 0.5%, 1.82% & 1.89%. When you look at most ETFs online, you'll find the fee on the first page. It can take a little more work to find the fee detail for mutual funds. That tells you something right there. You'll also find different series of mutual fund units or shares. Some series have lower fund fees, but these are typically only available through an advisor. You must pay the advisor first, who can then buy the cheap version for you. With the higher fee mutual fund examples mention above, all track the very same index as Vanguard's VFV, which comes with a MER of 0.09%. That's a huge difference in cost for tracking the very same index.

Yes, it is more challenging to set up a brokerage account & do your own ETF buying. Yes, you lose the hand holding that comes from having an advisor. But run the numbers through your compound growth calculator & see if the extra effort is worth it. If you invest both ways, managed & DIY, compare the results from both portfolios. You can put something into the mutual fund that your advisor is steering you towards & go solo with an ETF that matches that strategy. Then compare the results going forward. You can think of those high fees as the cost of your education! Or, for funds tracking the same index, it is easy to assess the advantage of going with a low-cost ETF. Just pull out your compound growth calculator & check the difference for yourself.

If you are helping an older family member review their investments, please don't encourage them to dump all their mutual funds in favour of ETFs. For starters, they might take a big capital gains hit. More importantly, some older investors cherish their relationship with their advisor. The handholding, the reassurances, & the cashflow management provided by their advisor makes them happy. All those things add value for them. But you could join them for the annual portfolio review with their advisor. Asking some questions might help get their fees reduced. While still allowing them to remain with an advisor they trust.

Now, let's get back to our conversation on diversification.

3. Go Global

When it comes to portfolio construction, diversity is a highly valued attribute. Diversification is a defence against ignorance. If I could pick stocks that I knew would win, I wouldn't worry about diversification. If I could pick the winning market every year, I'd just go with that market's index ETF each year. If I knew exactly when bonds were going to beat stocks, I'd go all in on bonds while that happened. If I could only tell the future, eh! But I can't do any of those things. So, instead, I diversify.

Our original ETF selections are limiting the diversity to the American & Canadian markets. While many of the companies contained in these funds operate globally, many experts say it's not enough. And that we need exposure to developed & emerging markets around the world too. No surprise this: there are ETFs that do all that for us now. Vanguard offers VEQT, BMO has ZEQT, & BlackRock's version is the iShares® XEQT. I'm going to use XEQT, the iShares® Core Equity ETF Portfolio, as the example here. It is large & liquid, which means that lots of shares trade every day, so you can usually sell some shares quickly, should you need to do that. The fund fee is 0.2%, which is pretty good for Canada. This ETF holds four other iShares® total market ETFs on the inside, with exposure to about 10,000 companies around the world. About 45% is allocated to the America market, approximately 25% to Canada, another 25% goes to developed countries, with less than 5% allocated to emerging or other markets. They don't double-dip on fees, the top line fee covers everything. Watch out for this any time you look at an ETF filled with other ETFs. Not all EFTs blend the fees like XEQT & the Vanguard & BMO ETFs mentioned above. When the company managing an ETF of ETFs is responsible for all the ETFs inside, the fees are usually blended into the topline fee. They don't double dip. You might find an ETF provider offering a fund that contains ETFs from other fund companies where this is not the case. You are then paying two sets of fees. The lower layer may be nested & hidden within the fund & the true cost might not show up in the topline fee numbers. But you may be paying both.

The XEQT ETF is a very clean & simple solution for a globally diversified portfolio, in just one fund. It even caters to our home country bias. Canada gets a bigger chunk than our percentage of the world's markets would suggest. There are some potential benefits & efficiencies to owning domestic stocks. Canadian dividends, for example, are tax-advantaged inside an ETF too. But how does this ETF perform against the S&P 500® index-tracking ETFs? Since these Canadian-listed ETFs are new, they don't have enough history to make a direct comparison over more than a couple of years. But we can look at the four underlying ETFs in XEQT & compare each of those to the performance of the S&P

500® index over a longer period. The following table shows the results, with all dividends reinvested, for 9 years. All the constituent ETFs have underperformed the S&P 500 Index® over that time. Look at the CAGR column. CAGR means Compound Annual Growth Rate. It's like the annual interest rate when we look backwards at investment performance.

Comparison XEQT vs "The Markets" 2014 - 2022			
ETF	Description	10k Return	CAGR
VFV (Can)	S&P 500 Index® in Canada	$31.6k	13.4%
SPY (US)	S&P 500 Index® in USA	$25.3k	10.7%
XIU (Can)	S&P/TSX 60 Index® in Canada	$19.4k	7.7%
ITOT (US)	XEQT Holding 45% (US Total Market)	$23.7k	10.1%
XIC (Can)	XEQT Holding 25% (Canada Composite Index)	$18.6k	7.2%
XEF (Can)	XEQT Holding 25% (Developed Markets)	$16.3k	5.6%
IEMG (US)	XEQT Holding 5% (Emerging Markets)	$11.8k	1.8%

Fig 3.3.1 Comparison XEQT vs "The Markets" 2014 – 2022

Note – IEMG was replaced by XEC in 2023. XEC previously held IEMG. It now holds emerging markets stocks directly. This is an improvement, as it reduces the impact of the dual layers of foreign withholding tax on a US-listed ETF inside a Canadian-listed ETF.

The first two rows both show the most popular American index, but VFV is the Canadian-listed version & SPY is a US-listed one. We'll look at those how those different currencies impact performance later. XIU is our Canadian top 60 index, for additional comparison. The bottom four rows show the XEQT holdings, with their percentage allocation in the description. A lower percentage holding will have a lower impact on the overall portfolio result. The 10k return column isn't matched to the allocation percentage, it's just for performance comparison between the four constituent ETFs. Two of them are US-listed, ITOT & IEMG, & the other two trade in Canada. Despite the promoted benefits of global & market cap diversification, at least in this example, the constituent ETFs have all underperformed the S&P 500® index over the past nine years. What gives? Where's the promised benefit of all the diversity & rebalancing stuff?

For starters, this timeline is far too short to tell what the long-term results might be. During this time, the S&P 500® index benefitted from a strong bull market. Over these years, low interest rates helped drive the growth of the big tech stocks that were dominating the US index. Things can change. Will the US market maintain its dominance going forward? Is it overvalued now? Will the small cap stocks in the total market funds outperform in the future? Who knows. But if the Canadian & International markets get their turns at a run of outperformance over the American market, this might be a great ETF to own. Many experts think there is value in being more diversified by geography & market cap size. If I were to get stranded on a desert island for a couple of decades, I'm guessing I'd be pretty pleased with the results from this ETF when I got back. It's important to remember that investing strategies can take a long time to prove their worth. Of course, we're not that well wired for patience!

Would you stick with Warren Buffett's bigger bet on

America? Maybe you'd like a little maple syrup on the side with that? Or should you go global for that greater diversity? It's worth noting that even Mr. Buffett is placing some bets outside America these days!

4. Rebalancing a Portfolio

Rebalancing is a simple concept. Imagine you have two ETFs in your portfolio. Over time, they each go up & down at different times. When these holdings get too far away from the planned balance, say it's 50:50 for simplicity, you sell some of the one that has grown to 55% of the portfolio. And buy more of the one that is now only 45%. The 50:50 balance is restored. Ideally, the two ETFs will take turns at leading the race. Rebalancing will sell the current winner & buy the current loser. That means that you are selling one at a high & buying the other at a low. When the balance changes, same thing happens in reverse. The new winner gets sold & the new loser gets bought. Rebalancing is usually done on a schedule. Many ETFs rebalance holdings on a six-monthly or annual basis. Or when an upper or lower allocation percentage limit is exceeded by one of the constituents.

Investors in individual stocks do something similar. They might have a cap on the weight that any one stock takes up in a portfolio. If a surging stock goes beyond its target weight of 3%, for example, some shares get sold off to bring it back under the investor's predefined limit. The money then gets redeployed to a stock that has fallen off the pace. This can pay off, but individual stocks take more work. When you own an ETF, the fund manager does all that rebalancing work for you.

Rebalancing is a good practice & it's an activity that can improve returns. You are, in theory, always selling high & buying low. That is a recipe for success. But it doesn't always work that way. If the ETFs in a portfolio don't take turns at winning & losing, there can be long stretches where a growing ETF is constantly being sold off in favour of an underperforming one. That will not improve returns during whatever length of time those trends sustain. And you can't tell how this is all going to work out for years. Maybe decades.

The Japanese stock market peaked in 1989 & it hasn't made it back to its all time high since then. Imagine an investor rebalancing a portfolio containing an American index fund & a Japanese index fund for the past 33 years. The winning American fund would have been sold off for most of those 33 years, to help rebalance the underperforming Japanese fund. With the expectation that it would be next year's better performer. That didn't happen much. While rebalancing away from the US market to many other markets didn't show much value over the past 10 or 15 years, it may matter in the future. Nobody can say for sure.

These global equity ETFs are a great example of how this works. The underlying ETFs target a fixed percentage of the holdings by geography & the fund manger ensures those percentages are maintained. If you like extra work, you could build your own portfolio of individual regional ETFs & you can play with the rebalancing yourself. Your trading costs would go up a bit, but the fees might be a little lower holding the individual ETFs. If you want that level of diversity, with professional rebalancing included, just buy an ETF like XEQT that does all that work for you.

One last thing to consider is the performance of some portfolios that are not rebalanced. Remember the Coffee Can Portfolio & those of the inactive investors who forgot they had a portfolio? Sometimes, just leaving things alone can work too. It's a little too pat to say that we should always let the winners run. While there are examples of where this proved to be true, it only works if you are lucky enough to have them running at the right time. And if you have some good winners in the mix.

Along with diversification, rebalancing is considered a free lunch in the investing world. Though it does add value over the long haul, it may give us a little indigestion over shorter time periods!

5. A Traditional Portfolio

Bonds are sneaky little guys. At a younger age, I saw them as an old person's investment. But there is a lot more going on with bonds than it appears at first glance. What are these bond things anyway?

Shareholders are owners, bond holders are loaners. Companies & government issues bonds. When you buy a bond, you are loaning money to the company. Or to federal, provincial, or regional governments. The government or company promises to pay interest, generally at a fixed rate (the coupon rate), on the loan. And they promise that you'll get all your money back at the end. That's a bond. And that fixed interest rate is why bonds are considered the "fixed income" part of a portfolio. Bonds are not risk free. While bond holders take priority over shareholders, you're not getting your money back if the company goes bust & there's no money left in the jar. The riskier the company, the higher the interest rate on the bonds. Chasing high bond yields can be as dangerous as chasing high yielding stocks. Government bonds, usually the most secure, tend to pay less than corporate bonds.

Traditional portfolio construction says that you ought to have a percentage of bonds in your portfolio. In general, the bond allocation is roughly matched to the decade of life the investor is in. A twenty-something would be invested in 20% bonds & a sixty-something would have 60%, & so on. The bond percentage increases by age because bonds are considered safer than stocks. Older people tend to want a portfolio & an income stream with more security & less risk. So older investors tend to hold more bonds. Declining interest rates over the past couple of decades have served the bond resale market well. Lower interest rates increase the value of an existing bond that pays a higher rate. On the other hand, if interest rates go up, the value of existing bonds go down. Not so nice should you want to sell. But if you hold a bond to maturity (the end of its term), along with getting the fixed coupon rate all the way through, you get all your money back at the end. The low interest rates since the 2008 financial crisis drove down the coupon rate on new bonds. For retirees living on fixed income, the lower bond yields made it more difficult for them to get a decent income stream from bonds or bond funds. But that's not the only value of bonds.

For the most part, bonds were somewhat inversely correlated with the stock market. When stocks went down, bonds went up. Or we at least hoped they didn't go down too. This works great for the rebalancing approach. Historically, stocks & bonds took turns being in & out of favour often enough to gain some advantage from rebalancing. That approach led to a buy-low, sell-high effect on both sides of the portfolio. When things worked like that, the traditional portfolio worked well. Despite the downward interest rate pressures created by central bank policies, there is still a strong case to be made for the returns on a portfolio holding both stocks *and* bonds. The risk-adjusted return can be better. That means you get still get a decent return, but with a little less of the roller-coaster ride that is typical of a pure stock portfolio. While bonds are generally more stable, stocks have provided better returns over time. When the market crashes, having bonds in a portfolio can help soften the blow. Your typical 60:40 stocks-to-bonds ratio is considered a "balanced" portfolio. The bonds provided downside protection when the market tanked. But in 2022, the bond market decided to take the biggest nosedive in the history of the bond market. Thanks to rapidly rising interest rates. Unfortunately, that happened at the same time as the stock market decided to go south. That's one of the things you'll learn about investing: just when you think you have it all figured out, it goes & does something completely different. And nobody knows what's coming next.

There are investors who shun bonds completely. I don't think that's the right thing to do. With today's low bond yields, a younger investor might see less value in bonds. You are basically buying some small degree of stability, to help get you though periods of stock market volatility. With stocks *and* bonds going down in 2022, it didn't work so well over that short timeframe. But if interest rates rise sufficiently, there may be a lengthy period where central banks will work to reduce them again. And that could be good for bonds & bond funds. As you figure out what percentage of bonds you might like to hold, the first question you need to ask yourself is this ... can you handle the volatility of an all-equity portfolio? And you also need to think about the potential benefits of rebalancing on the long-term outcome. That can make a difference too.

A big part of your learning experience is going be figuring out how well you'll manage those challenges. If you think you'll panic when your shiny new $20k portfolio suddenly gets cut in half, imagine how you'll feel 30 years from now if your million-dollar portfolio drops by a half a million dollars! Will you be able to handle that kind of drop? Now, if you can imagine being able to weather all that volatility well, then you can probably work with a lower bond allocation. At least while you are younger. But if you think you'll do better with a bond safety net, add bonds. It is reasonable to reduce risk by increasing the bond percentage as you age. And as the value of your portfolio grows.

Fortunately, there are single ETF solutions that do all this for us too. Many fund providers offer a range of asset allocation portfolios that include bonds. They have Growth, Balanced & Conservative ETFs where the GRO version is typically about 20% bonds, the BAL has 40% & the CON (or CNS) jumps to 60% bonds for older or more conservative investors. Check out ZGRO, VGRO, & XGRO, for examples of all-in-one funds with a 20% bond allocation. These are solutions that give you a globally diversified equity allocation, combined with diversified bond funds. All you do is match one to the age & stage of life you are at. Or to your risk tolerance. All come with reasonable fees for Canadian offerings. They are rebalanced by the ETF managers, so you don't have to worry about any of that. These are good solutions. It's an entire, complete, & pretty sophisticated portfolio all wrapped up in a single ETF.

If, instead, you choose to go with the index-tracking ETFs for the US & Canada, there might be one other reason to hold a separate bond fund while you are young. You would have something to sell during a market crash. You can use the proceeds from selling off some of the bond fund to add more of your now-on-sale index ETFs. You could allocate 10% of your portfolio to a bond ETF, for example. Do you remember which great investor recommended that bond allocation? Of course, Mr. Buffett's ability to navigate turbulent markets is a proven strength. Ours might not be!

If bond ETF yields are lower than current bank interest rates, putting some cash into a high yield savings account is a good alternative. Or go into one of those newer ETFs that do that for you. Horizons, Purpose Investments, CI Financial, BMO, & others, have cash-like or high interest savings ETFs that cover this off. Then you'll have something to sell when the markets fall off a cliff & your favourite equity ETFs are on sale. I'm not promoting market timing here, this is rebalancing. And the advantage of rebalancing during a crash is that you'll be focused on the rebalancing exercise. Instead of thinking you should be selling everything in a panic. Rebalancing to buy good stuff cheap usually doesn't hurt a portfolio.

If you have a safe & substantial pension to look forward to in retirement, you could reduce the bond allocation from what would be considered appropriate for your age. If you can live comfortably on that pension, you might be able to tolerate the greater volatility & risk of a higher equity allocation in your portfolio. In the hope that it will lead to greater reward over time.

I'm sorry to muddy the waters more for you, but the choice is now yours. Start out with the all-equity ETFs? Or maybe you want an ETF that holds a position in bond funds? Unfortunately, becoming a more sophisticated investor means you must make these decisions for yourself. If you want a sophisticated solution with bonds, but without any work, then go with one of the all-in-one asset allocation funds.

One last thing. Bonds look simple & straightforward, but they are not. They are highly nuanced. As is the plan you'd need to put in place for purchasing individual bonds. Buying individual bonds leads you into a maze of laddering. You'll need a large enough selection for diversity. With different yields & durations. They need to mature at different dates & as one matures, you need to be prepared to replace it. You'll have to figure out how they interact with interest rate trends. There's a lot more learning here than it appears at first glance. Bonds are anything but simple. And this adds more work to the portfolio management process. I don't understand the bond market well enough to do all that work so I use low-cost bond ETFs instead. It's easier.

6. Best Time to Buy

Starting out with small regular investment amounts, the best time to buy is now. Right now, right away, as soon as the automatic savings transfer happens. Imagine you bought one share of your ETF last month for $100 & the market crashes 50% just when you're about to buy this month's share. Now, instead of one, you'll get two shares for $100. While the value of all your prior investments just plummeted by 50% from the peak, your favourite ETF just went on sale. Don't wait to see if it drops further next month, just follow your regular timing & process. Take advantage of this month's sale price. Now it won't feel good when it happens, but it's the younger investor that will benefit most from market downturns. The younger you are & the longer the downturn, the better it is for you. You get to buy more good stuff cheap. The more good stuff you get at lower cost, the greater the growth potential over time.

Until you've been through a few downturns & recoveries, this can be emotionally difficult to digest. It's tough to throw more money into the market when it feels like the world is on fire. But what happens if you don't? The $100 share you bought last month is only worth $50 after the crash. Historically, the market has always recovered. And then gone on to new highs. If you hold back the next $100 investment when the shares are on sale, you'll have a total of $200 when the recovery is complete. That's $100 in the original share, plus the $100 in sidelined cash. If you had taken the plunge & bought the two new shares at $50 each, they too will have doubled. The portfolio is then worth $300 after the recovery. The original share went back up to $100 & the two new shares you bought at $50 have now doubled to $100 each. Sticking with the process produced a better result. Don't fear the market turmoil, use it to your advantage. Note that this is not always so reliable an approach with individual stocks. Some stocks that crash, particularly outside of a broad market crash, don't recover so well. Sometimes not at all.

Over time, the markets will surge & crash. Most experts tell us this is just noise & we should ignore it. The long trend is up. We should carry on investing on our regular schedule, regardless of what the market is doing from day to day. Ironically, we retail investors tend to panic & sell closer to the bottom. Then we sit on the sidelines, worrying about the best time to get back in. While the recovery happens without us. Stick to your process. Nobody can time the market well. And certainly not consistently. Short of having a little luck, maybe not at any time. After all, active portfolio managers are, in theory, buying & selling the "right" stocks at the "right" time, all the time. Yet, most professionals cannot beat the average market returns over time.

The flip side of the above scenario is that the share price has increased since the last purchase. Since the market is going up more often than down, that's likely to happen more often, but the same rule applies. Just carry on buying on your regular schedule. Nobody can predict how long the next bull or bear market will last. Nobody can predict market tops or bottoms. Not even the pros. For most of us, sticking with a process of saving & investing regularly & consistently works better. But if there is a sudden big crash, there's nothing wrong with doing some impromptu rebalancing with your bond funds. Or with going into the couch cushions to round up any extra loose change that might be invested while things are on sale!

What if you have a lump sum to invest, should you invest it all at once? Logically, mathematically, & based on almost all the probability studies out there, the answer is yes. I must admit that I would find that very difficult. All the studies say do it. Invest everything right away. But I just couldn't bring myself to throw all the money in at once. Especially if the pundits are all saying that the market is overvalued. That it's at all-time highs. And that there must be a big crash round the corner. I know I am allowing my emotions to get in the way of what the numbers say we should do. But I just can't pull the trigger & dump everything in at once.

You need to create your own rules for when you get into a situation like this. In other words, you'll need a process for handling this too. Some will invest one third right away, another third one month or one quarter later, with the final third the next month or next quarter. If the amount is larger, maybe you'll want to spread it over a longer time. We're not all wired the same way. Define your process ahead of time & be ready to follow it.

On top of all these mental challenges, I find it easier to ignore the noise when I'm investing in an ETF, rather than in individual stocks. The risk is diversified across multiple stocks in an ETF, so I don't have to worry about evaluating & comparing several individual companies, to find the "best" one for the current market conditions. That's a great paralysing excuse too. And another reason why ETFs are often both psychologically & financially better for many investors.

Aside from trying to take advantage of an occasional market crash to rebalance, steer clear of market timing. Even when retail investors only invest in index funds, ducking in & out is what causes most of us to further underperform the market.

Invest regularly, follow your process, & tune out the noise.

7. Gains, Income & Taxes

This & the following three chapters all come with a TAX WARNING. This is not tax advice & tax laws change constantly, so you **must** check out the tax implications of your investment choices & the location of those investments on your own. If you can't do it yourself, work with a tax specialist. Get professional advice. Here, we'll hit some of the highlights, so you have some idea of what to look out for. The whole purpose of investing is to make money. When we make money, we want to keep as much of it as possible. Let's look at the basic ways we can make money on our investments.

Capital Gains

Capital gains happen when we sell an investment for more than it cost us to buy it. Capital gains are sheltered in a TFSA & RRSP. In an RRSP, the growth is sheltered, but subsequent withdrawals are taxed at our marginal rate. In a taxable account, we are currently taxed on only 50% of the capital gains.

What makes for a capital gain? If we buy a stock for $100 & pay a trading commission of $10, our book value or adjusted cost base (ACB) is now $110.00. When we sell the stock for $200.00, we pay another $10 trading fee. The difference between all our costs $120 (100 + 10 + 10 = 120) & our selling price of $200 is $80. That's the capital gain. In a taxable account, we only pay taxes on 50% of the gain, or on $40 of the $80 gain. If we sell another position at a loss, the capital losses can be offset against capital gains. If there are no capital gains to be offset, capital losses are held on our CRA account to be offset against future capital gains. You can't play games in a taxable account by selling something to create a capital loss & then buy it back right away. Nor can your spouse buy it back right away. Look up the superficial loss rule. Since capital gains are protected in sheltered accounts, capital losses inside the RRSP & TFSA accounts cannot be offset. Day trading is considered to be a business by the CRA & you can't do that in a TFSA, gains can be treated as income for tax purposes.

Dividend Income (Canadian)

For most working taxpayers, dividend income from Canadian-listed stocks & funds is the next best way to make money. Since the company has already paid taxes on the profits that give us the dividend, we get a dividend tax credit to reduce the amount of tax we pay. There are eligible & non-eligible dividends. Eligible dividends come from companies that have already paid their full taxes on profits. Non-eligible dividends might come from a small company that only pays tax at the reduced small business tax rate, so we get a reduced dividend tax credit. At lower income levels, if dividends make up most of your income, Canadian dividends can win out as the most tax-efficient form of income. Younger investors are still accumulating & reinvesting those dividends. Though automatically reinvesting the dividends makes it feel like you never had the dividends in your hands, you'll still pay tax on them in a taxable account. For retirees with larger dividend income, the

CRA gross up calculation on Canadian dividend income can inflate the gross income number for the retiree & that can result in OAS clawback. Note that not all distributions are dividends. You'll need to visit the company's or fund's website to see a breakdown of the tax classification of the distributions. And that changes from one year to the next.

Interest Income

Interest income is a poorer way to make money, from a tax perspective. It is added on top of the wages from our day job & it is taxed at our marginal tax rate in a taxable account. Interest income comes from a bank savings account, GICs, bonds, & bond funds. Some ETF distributions may include an interest component.

Dividend Income (Foreign)

Dividend income from foreign sources is treated as ordinary income & is taxed at the taxpayer's marginal rate. Just like interest income. Foreign dividends take another hit because the foreign country will apply a dividend withholding tax in the country of origin. The rate varies by country but the standard US dividend withholding tax is 30%. Under the current US-Canada tax treaty, that goes down to 15%. But you need to have a current W-8BEN on file with your brokerage to avail of that. If you have US equities that pay a dividend, call your brokerage to ensure you do. Currently, this document must be renewed every 3 years. There is no dividend tax credit from the CRA on US or other foreign dividends, but there is a foreign tax credit to counter the withholding tax. This foreign tax credit isn't as good as the Canadian dividend tax credit. But it does mean that we don't pay the same tax twice. Otherwise, the income is treated as ordinary income.

Return of Capital (ROC)

Some ETFs give us our own money back. This is called Return of Capital, or ROC. If the fund is reducing the net asset value, the NAV, of the fund to sustain a monthly payout then that's true. We really are getting our own money back. That's usually a bad thing for the future value of the shares. Some ROC distributions come from the internal workings of the fund, not from giving us our own money back. With this, the underlying value doesn't take a direct hit. You'll hear this referred to as "good" ROC. Regardless of the type, ROC distributions will show up in a separate section of our tax slips & they have a deferred tax impact. They will change the Adjusted Cost Base (ACB), or book value, of our investments. That means we'll have a bigger capital gain amount when we eventually sell the shares. Unfortunately, the tax slips don't tell us if we're getting good or bad ROC. We must work at finding that out on the fund's website & it's not easy. Sometimes impossible. But from a tax perspective, all ROC results in an adjusted cost base that increases capital gains when shares are eventually sold.

Next, we'll look at the accounts & how to use them.

8. Accounts

We're going to focus on the Tax-Free Savings Account (TFSA), the Registered Retirement Savings Plan (RRSP), & a taxable (non-registered) account, sometimes referred to as a cash or margin account. If you plan on buying a home, look at the recently announced First Home Savings Account (FHSA) too. This looks like an interesting account for anyone that hasn't owned a home in the past 4 years. Even if you don't plan to buy a home, this might be a good account to open. It provides a tax deduction like an RRSP, & you can take all your money out tax-free, like a TFSA, but **only** to buy a home. If you decide you don't want a home, you can take it out & pay tax on it like regular income. Or you can move it into your RRSP, so it's like free extra RRSP room. It's still new, so keep an eye out for ongoing changes to the rules, but it looks like a great account to fire up.

Tax Free Savings Account (TFSA)
The TFSA is awesome. It is the only totally tax-free account we have. We don't get a refund from our contributions but, outside of day trading income, we **never** have to pay Canadian taxes on anything we grow or earn inside this account. There are no taxes due on anything we withdraw from this account & we get the contribution room back. In addition to protecting capital gains from taxes, all Canadian interest & dividends are accumulated, tax-free, inside the TFSA.

Make sure it's set up to roll to your spouse's TFSA under the TFSA umbrella, in case you die. Don't let it cash out if you have a spouse. There would be no tax liability for the survivor, but the sheltering of future growth on the deceased's portfolio would be gone. Check your brokerage signup paperwork to see which box you checked.

There are some disadvantages. We cannot write off any capital losses inside the TFSA. If we sell a losing stock or ETF, we take the full hit. Since the capital gains from selling a winning position are tax free, we can't offset a capital loss. In other words, it's good for growth, but maybe not for speculating or gambling. Unless you get really lucky! The other disadvantage is that dividends from American-listed & foreign stocks, & ETFs with foreign holdings, are all subject to withholding taxes. And no foreign tax credit can be applied here.

There are contribution limits & operational limits on all registered accounts. You can **not** day-trade in a TFSA. The CRA looks at day trading as a business & it's not allowed. Gains will be treated as income & taxed. Though the definitions seem a little vague, be careful with this. You can't take money out of a TFSA one day & pop it back in the next either. Your contribution room will be increased by the withdrawal amount, but you must wait 'til the following calendar year to put it back in. There are CRA penalties for all transgressions. Not knowing the rules is not a good excuse. Read the CRA website for all the current rules & limitations. Once you've done your taxes & received your Notice of Assessment, check this & your CRA My Account for your contribution limits. You can have as many TFSA accounts as you like, but the contribution limits apply to the total amount of all contributions to all TFSA accounts. There is no such thing as a joint TFSA account. You & your spouse each get your own. But designate your spouse to get the account rolled over, with the tax-sheltering intact, should you depart. If you had a TFSA account before you got married, go & have those instructions updated.

Registered Retirement Savings Plan (RRSP)
The RRSP is a great account to crank up in the early years too. Again, there are annual contribution limits, spelled out on your Notice of Assessment from the CRA. This is only accurate if you, your employer, & your financial institutions have reported all your earnings & contributions accurately. That is usually the case, but the onus is always on the taxpayer when it comes to reporting everything to the CRA. The contribution limits to an RRSP are 18% of last year's earned income, subject to a maximum limit, currently around $31k. Interest & dividend income in a taxable account are not earned income, so you can't boost your RRSP contribution room with income from investments. The RRSP is not a tax-free account, instead it is a tax-deferred account. When you take money out in retirement, it's taxable. Any time you take money out of your RRSP account, it's taxable as income. And you can't recover the contribution room. There are exceptions if you borrow from your RRSP for specific education &

home-buying programs. But you must complete the official forms if you want to use these facilities. And you must pay the money back to your RRSP within the program guidelines. On the bright side, RRSP contributions are tax-deductible & we get a refund for contributing to the plan. You can modify your tax contributions so that you are not "loaning" some of your money to the government until tax refund time. Many taxpayers don't bother to do this. Despite the lost opportunity cost, logical or not, everyone loves a refund.

Non-Registered (Taxable, Margin or Cash) Account

The greatest tax pain may be experienced in a regular investing account. This is not tax-sheltered in any way. We pay taxes on everything we make. Though it does provide the comfort of being able to offset losses against gains. Don't fall foul of the superficial loss rule by selling a losing investment & buying it back again right away. And we get the foreign tax credit to help offset foreign withholding taxes here. Canadian dividend income benefits from the better Canadian dividend tax credit.

9. Which Account is Best?

Since keeping more of our money is the goal, the tax-sheltered accounts are best to start with. The TFSA & RRSP are both great but where should you start? In an ideal world, you'd be able to max out both accounts every year but that's a pipe dream for a lot of us. We've already looked at the tax-free versus tax-deferred nature of these accounts, but we still need to pick the best one to invest in starting out.

The simple way to look at it is this: if you're paying little or no tax on your income, go with the TFSA. If you're in a higher tax bracket, go more towards the RRSP & put your refund into the TFSA. A very general guideline is to stick with the TFSA up to around $50k in annual income. Above $80k, it's more likely to be the RRSP. Then put your refunds back into the TFSA. This is very general. There are too many variations in personal circumstances to pick the "right" strategy for everyone. Someone with education & tuition deductions might earn more than $50k but pay very little tax, for example. Paying little tax means little or no refund, so the TFSA might be the better choice here. For anyone with a group RRSP through work, the focus might be more towards the TFSA for additional personal savings. If you have expectations of a higher salary going forward, you might want to save the RRSP contribution room for those higher earning years. When you'll get a bigger refund. There's just too much stuff here to pick a one-size-fits-all solution. However, that often leads to paralysis. Don't get so caught up in figuring out the "best" answer that you can't make any decision at all. If you can't make up your mind, split your investable savings between the two & get on with it. If you do want to dig into it a little more, you could use your favourite tax preparation software to see what different scenarios look like. Just don't mistakenly submit the returns while you are checking things out. Wealthsimple Tax has a practice account where you can play around & optimise the choice, without fear of doing that.

There is a psychological choice to be made here too. If you are going to raid your TFSA for a trip to the sunny south every year, go with the RRSP instead! On the other hand, if you have spare TFSA contribution room that you don't expect to get caught up on in the coming years, there's no reason not to put your fun money in here too. Just be conscious of the difference between the long-term investments & the fun money. Though I encourage you to see the TFSA as a long-term investing account, it might also be a good place for your emergency fund in the early years. If you have spare TFSA contribution room that you know you can't use right away, why not use it store & grow your emergency fund tax-free. You'll need to make different investment choices with your emergency fund money, of course. You don't want an investment that falls in value for your emergency money. And any emergency fund investment must be very liquid. It needs to be immediately convertible to cash when the emergency strikes. An emergency can't wait for a one-year GIC to mature.

Emergency fund considerations aside, don't make too big a meal of deciding between the TFSA & RRSP accounts. Doing nothing is one of the biggest issues for a new investor. If you have money that you are sure you won't need for decades, you should invest it. The latest data from Statistics Canada says that a little over 15 million Canadians have a TFSA account. There are almost 30 million adults in Canada now, so what are the other 15 million folk doing? And of the 15 million that have a TFSA account, only about 10% of those accounts are maxed out. If you can't make up your mind, just start off with a TFSA & keep loading it up while you figure things out.

Are we there yet? Not quite, we still have the taxable investing account to consider. I can't think of too many reasons to invest in a taxable account if you still have spare contribution room in a tax-sheltered account. If you want a small portfolio to speculate with, the taxable account can work for that. If you are lucky enough to max out your sheltered accounts, then you will need to invest here. And that brings a whole bunch of other complications to the table. We'll look at some of the implications of investing in a taxable account in the next chapter.

10. What's Best for Each Account?

This is another situation where getting bogged down in details can stop us making decisions. While we'll cover some of the pitfalls, the work & costs involved with avoiding some of them can outweigh the benefits for many. Simplicity often wins out if concern for the details leads to doing nothing.

If you go with a simple global equity or all-in-one ETF strategy, you have already solved most of your complexity problems. Buy that ETF in the TFSA & RRSP accounts. Even if you are buying two or three ETFs, there is nothing wrong with buying those same ETFs across all registered accounts. Yes, we can be dinged for those foreign withholding taxes, but how big a deal is that?

Those equity & all-in-one ETFs pay out pretty small distributions. If you look at the tax distribution data on the funds' websites, ballpark, it might result in a tax drag of something between 0.15 to 0.25% in sheltered accounts. That's going to cost you between $150 & $250 for each one hundred-thousand-dollars invested. You can't buy much tax advice for 250 bucks. Regardless of how much you pay, it's unlikely the tax advice will be able to recover 100% of the tax drag. Or possibly not without sacrificing diversity. Some of the tax avoidance strategy might require buying US-listed equities in the RRSP. The foreign currency transaction costs will wipe out the tax advantage in the average portfolio for a couple or several years. Bottom line is that you shouldn't worry too much about the tax drag implications in these low yielding funds. For a big enough portfolio, over a long enough timeframe, those costs can magnify & that might justify taking action. The RRSP account is the only place to avoid US withholding taxes. But that applies only to US-listed equities. And that means you're back to figuring in the cost of currency exchange & US tax reporting exposure. Here's a quick overview summary of the exposures from different investments.

Canadian-listed Stocks & ETFs holding Canadian Stocks
These work well across all accounts. No tax exposure in TFSA or RRSP accounts, other than not being able to claim capital losses. Eligible Canadian dividends are favourably taxed in a taxable account, & capital gains taxes apply when shares are sold at a gain.

Canadian-listed ETFs holding US Stocks & ETFs
Foreign dividend withholding taxes are applied inside the fund & they cannot be recovered in tax-sheltered accounts. In a taxable account there is a foreign withholding tax credit that offsets paying that tax twice. This isn't as good as the Canadian dividend tax credit, but it helps.

Canadian-listed ETFs holding non-US Stocks & ETFs
Foreign dividend withholding taxes apply & cannot be recovered in tax-sheltered accounts. In a taxable account there is a foreign withholding tax credit that can offset paying that tax twice. Canadian ETFs that hold ETFs of foreign stocks listed on the US exchanges lose the ability to offset the lower layer of foreign

withholding tax. Choose Canadian-listed ETFs that hold the foreign stocks directly.

US-listed stocks & ETFs holding only US stocks

The RRSP, RRIF & LIRA accounts ("official" retirement accounts) avoid the foreign dividend withholding tax, the TFSA does not. The foreign withholding tax credit offsets this only in a taxable account.

US-listed ETFs holding other foreign stocks & ETFs

This is another layer of foreign withholding tax. Those other foreign countries withhold tax from the US & they cannot be recovered in Canada. We only get to offset the US withholding tax component up here.

While every small cost & drag will compound negatively over the years, avoiding these issues comes with a drag too. You have to weigh up the costs & value of trying to avoid them. It does take time & effort. And it will involve investing on the US exchanges, in US dollars. Unless you want to spend time figuring it all out, most of us will do fine with those single ETF portfolio solutions. Though we will dig into the whole currency thing a little more in the next chapter.

11. Currency Exchange Costs & Hedging

Vanguard offers virtually identical S&P 500® index funds in the US & Canada. The Buffett-recommended VOO version trades in the US, while VFV & VSP trade in Toronto. VFV was created for the Canadian market & does exactly what VOO does. The VSP fund is identical, but it is hedged to protect against currency fluctuations. The American VOO has an expense ratio of 0.03%, while both Canadian funds charge 0.09%. Things always seem to cost more in Canada but those are still reasonable.

The table below shows the results of $10k invested in each of these ETFs from November 2012 to May 2022. Remember, they all track the same index. But the relative performance looks very different.

Ticker	CAGR %	$10k
VFV	16.6%	$43k
VOO	14.1%	$35k
VSP	13.0%	$32k

What's going on here? How can three Vanguard funds, all tracking the same index, perform so differently?

I used the total returns for comparison, with dividends reinvested. Over nine & a half years, VOO turned $10k into almost $36k, while VFV vaulted a $10k investment to $43k. The currency hedged VSP showed the poorest result here. If you're thinking that VFV is the obvious choice, hang on a minute.

Back in November 2012, the US & Canadian dollar were at par. By the end of this comparison, the Canadian dollar was worth about 79 cents American. Divide the VOO return of $35k, which is US dollars, by 0.79 & you get … wait for it … $44k Canadian! That's about what you'd expect, a slight outperformance by VOO, because of its lower fee & without applying the withholding tax to the dividend. The hedged version did the poorest. There is an added cost for the fund manager to hedge currencies & it's hard to tell how well they will hedge. It doesn't look great for the hedged version in this example, over this timeline. By not using hedged versions, we must put up with the consequences of the swings in the exchange rates. Exchange rates don't adhere to a regular schedule but, over a long enough time horizon, things seem to balance out. It may not be worth the drag of the hedging costs. Though hedging may provide protection against crazy fluctuations, should something totally go off the rails, I favour the non-hedged ETFs. Over the time span for this table, the Canadian dollar was generally weakening against the US dollar & that gave a big numerical, not value, advantage to VFV. This wouldn't have been the case if the loonie gone up over time.

What does it all mean?

VOO looks like a marginal winner for a long-term, buy-and-hold investment inside an RRSP account, where it is protected from withholding tax on the dividends. But there are still currency exchange costs to consider. We need to convert our loonies to US dollars to buy VOO & there is a cost for doing that. We pay currency exchange fees to convert back again if we want to spend the proceeds in Canada. Outside of an RRSP account, that withholding tax protection for VOO vanishes. VFV, by comparison, only saves on currency exchange fees. Though those costs can be in the 1 to 2% range for individual investors, & that's not insignificant. The slightly higher MER would disadvantage VFV against VOO over the long haul. But not by enough to put me off buying it. I prefer to pay a little more to avoid the tax reporting implications of owning US-listed equities. And for avoiding the currency exchange costs. I sacrifice some return for simplicity. Anyone who wants to hold US-listed equities should check out Norbert's Gambit for a more cost-effective way to do currency exchange. Especially for larger amounts. There is a return advantage to buying the US-listed ETF for a larger investment over a longer investment timeline. You'll have to decide if it's worth the effort for you.

It was a happy coincidence that the US & Canadian dollar were at par for the start date of this comparison. Starting the same exercise today, with the Canadian dollar worth 79 cents American, you'd need to buy Can$12,658.00 of VFV to match the US$10k buy of VOO. In the example above, the CAGR numbers show not only the growth of share price appreciation, but also the numeric gains derived from the Canadian dollar decline against the US dollar over that period. The difference between VFV & VOO is pretty small when you consider currency exchange rates at the beginning & end. Had the Canadian dollar continued to appreciate over the US dollar during that time, the Canadian VFV return numbers would have been lower. But worth more when converted to US dollars at the end. Currency hedging is protection from changes in the relative strength of the loonie versus the greenback over time. In this instance, VSP didn't work out very well. I'm guessing due to the hedging costs that happen inside the fund. And the inability of anyone to perfectly time hedging over time.

If this all hurts your head, think of it another way. You know how Canadians love to visit America when our dollar is at par with the greenback? Why do we do that? Because our loonie is now buying much more American stuff than we typically get. The lineups at the border get longer, more of us take trips to Florida, & online shopping & shipping from the US goes up. It's the same with stocks. Investing is just like cross-border shopping, you get more American stuff for fewer loonies when the loonie is at par. Buying VFV when the loonie was high helped produce the winning result in the table above.

Over the past 20 or more years, the average exchange rate is around 80 cents US for a Canadian dollar. If the exchange rate is above 80 cents American for a loonie, you might do a little better buying American than if it were below. However, waiting for currency exchange rates to change before you buy your Canadian-listed American index fund is probably not wise. You could lose out on a whole lot of market growth waiting for that to happen. If things got crazily out of whack between the currencies, I might pause & try to figure out what's going on. I might shift my investing bias for new money at extreme valuations. But in the 70 to 90 cents range, I would carry on buying with my regular process & not even think about it. It's a dollar cost averaging approach to the ever-changing currency exchange rate. The bottom line is that you can grow your wealth in either currency. And most things even out & come back to the middle over time. Including currency exchange rates.

Outside of the differences in return, there are Canadian tax reporting requirements if you own combined foreign property that cost more than Can$100,000.00 outside of registered accounts. Foreign property includes US-listed stocks. If you pass that total cost value any time during the year, you need to report it to the CRA. Right now, the requirement is to complete the T1135 form. The CRA currently doesn't mind if we own more. But we must tell them about it. That cost number also applies if you ever get around to buying a condo in Florida. When it comes to US tax reporting, the bigger worry might be for your heirs. Currently, there are IRS tax reporting requirements for Canadians that pass away, while owning more than US$60,000 worth of American-listed equities at market value on the day of death. And potential US estate tax liability if you have really big bucks (many millions currently, but that can change) invested in the US market & in US real estate. All of this is beyond the scope here, so you'll need to speak to a cross-border tax professional if you are more heavily invested in American property & stocks. But if you don't want to leave a spouse or the inheritors of your estate with a US tax reporting & exposure situation to sort out, you might want to limit exposure to US-listed equities. Most (not sure if there are exceptions) Canadian-listed ETFs that hold American stocks are not considered foreign property.

Many investors like US-listed equities but, for simplicity, I remain a lazy loonie lover for the most part!

12. Estimates & Inflation

I have taken the easy road with most of my calculations & numbers throughout. I have ignored inflation. It keeps thing simple & most of my calculations present tomorrow's estimates as though they had today's value. In estimating the future value of a portfolio, for example, a million dollars today will be worth a lot less in real terms forty years from now. However, the idea of investing the equivalent of one hour's work a week means that we ignore the growth of wages over those same forty years too. There will be different spreads between the growth of wages & inflation over time. But if you carry on saving a certain number of hours worth of wages a week 'til retirement, your hourly rate will go up over time too. You should be saving far more dollars per hour of work forty years from now, compared to today. Wage growth won't be a perfect match with inflation, but for the purposes of explanation & ease of comparison it works well enough. Back in the real world, we do need to give inflation some attention, especially when it comes to retirement income. But we'll get to that in a bit.

13. Are You Sophisticated Yet?

If you have friends that are making gobs of money in crypto or with the latest high-flying tech stock, your index investing strategy can feel quite boring. Take a breath & hold on. Know that you are following the advice of some of the world's truly most sophisticated investors & economists. Sophistication in investing is not about temporary bragging rights. It's about the long-term compounding of wealth. If you invest everything in just one of the all-equity ETFs, for example, you can confidently say that you have a globally diversified portfolio. One that embraces large, mid, & small cap equities. Across all the appropriate industry classification sectors. And that you rebalance annually, to ensure adherence to your asset allocation model. That's the XEQT, VEQT, ZEQT type ETFs & that is some pretty sophisticated investing right there. If you want to add bonds to the mix, go with VGRO, ZGRO or XGRO instead. And then you can tack on some blather about "the improved risk-adjusted returns of a portfolio with a bond allocation" to your spiel at the coffee shop. Tell me that won't impress your friends!

You may only be buying one ETF but, under the hood, it is quite the sophisticated portfolio. However, in the next section we're going to look at some things that might mess up this beautifully simple approach!

Part 4 – How to Pick Great Stocks

If you think I can deliver on this headline, you haven't been paying attention! We are going to explore stock picking in this section. But, by the time we're done, I'm hoping you'll have a better understanding of how challenging that can be. Despite the challenges, many of us can't help dabbling. For when the impulse strikes, we'll cover one strategy that might keep you safer.

In addition to the stock strategy we cover in this section, we'll look at some interesting tools that are good for monitoring & comparing stocks. If you want to quickly skim the stock picking chapters, that's okay. But don't ignore the tools. These tools are very useful for comparing ETFs too. And you can compare the past performance of a stock portfolio to a simple ETF portfolio. This might tell you if it's worth spending all the extra time it takes to build & manage a stock portfolio. On top of that, these tools can help you figure out if you can retire early using the latest FIRE strategy that you're reading about online!

I think you'll find some of this interesting.

1. Why Stock Picking?

There are several approaches to stock picking. Some try to buy the stocks that will change the world & that seem to have unlimited growth potential. Others focus on whatever stocks or sectors that show the greatest momentum this year. There are those who like the idea of buying quality businesses. Or companies that have fallen on hard times. They'll almost certainly recover & go on to new highs, right? No matter the strategy, short of having insider knowledge (& trading on insider knowledge is illegal!) or really good luck, the average investor is usually the last to learn about something that will send their picks to the stratosphere. We are at the end of the information food chain & by the time we hear anything, it's probably already factored into the share price.

Usually, the whole idea behind stock picking is to beat the market. The average investor believes he, or she, can beat the average market returns by picking one or more stocks that will do just that. Some of the world's greatest investors have suggested we can't. If you recall the SPIVA® scorecard we mentioned earlier, neither can most of the professionals, most of the time.

So why do we do it?

We just can't help ourselves. Some of us are more prone than others to do it. The same way some of us go to the casino more often. Or we buy more lottery tickets than our friends. If the long shot comes off, we're on top of the world. It seems like the more desperate we are, the more likely we are to go for broke. And sometimes, going broke is the more likely outcome.

But what if we choose stocks for reasons other than beating the market?

2. Learning from Old People

Boomers didn't grow up with online trading & some have never transitioned fully to the new digital age. But many have. And as they learned, they started thinking differently about investing for retirement. Some of them got pretty good at it.

Retirees worry about some strange things. Like outliving their money in retirement. You'll find old people in cafés, huddled over their tablets & phones, muttering about Monte Carlo simulations & the 4% Rule. They're not planning a gambling trip to Europe; they're doing retirement planning. These tools aren't just for old people, you can use them to help put your financial plan together. Especially if you're a fan of the FIRE (Financial Independence, Retire Early) movement. Monte Carlo simulations use guidelines like the 4% rule to calculate the chances of a retiree, regardless of age, outliving their nest-egg. There are some trade-offs in retirement. You could live more frugally & have greater certainty of having money all the way to age 120. Or you could party like a wild thing & be pretty sure that you'll run out of money by age 80. If you are very confident that you won't make it past 80, & if you don't plan on leaving an inheritance, that's okay. Party on!

The 4% Rule was developed by a financial planner, William Bengen, back in the nineties. The basic idea is that you can withdraw 4% from the portfolio every year for retirement income. Increasing the withdrawal amount sufficiently each year to keep pace with inflation. Testing this rule with thousands of Monte Carlo simulations, the survival rate of a 50:50 American stock & bond portfolio under this rule was generally good. The idea caught on & this rule, or some variation of it, is widely used as part of retirement planning calculations now. Financial planners & advisors use tools like these to look at the probability of success for their clients. Success is measured by the chances of the investor still having money up to the day they die. You can do this too, with free tools that are available online. Now if you miscalculate, or if the markets don't co-operate, you might go broke before you kick the bucket.

You need to be careful with this. There are some further studies suggesting that the 4% withdrawal rate might be too aggressive nowadays. Due to increased longevity & the recent history of US market outperformance. The American market has returned almost 16% annually from 2009 to the end of 2021. That's far above the historical rate of return. Recent outperformance suggests that we might be in for a period of lower returns going forward. Things always seem to revert to the mean. That's means that what goes up must come back down, sooner or later. And things usually fall down further than the middle, before working their way back up again. The 4% Rule is less a rule & more a guideline. Depending on circumstances & market conditions, we might need to plan on being flexible with those withdrawal rates during retirement.

Let's get back to the older folk & their challenges. For retirees, their big problem with index funds is that they need to sell off some shares every year for income. After a lifetime of saving & investing, doing that can be a mental challenge for some. Especially when the markets are down. They would prefer to have a portfolio that delivers an income stream instead. One big enough to avoid ever having to sell shares. This is a big deal for anyone planning on leaving an inheritance for their kids too. If the 4% rule is anywhere close to being right, then a portfolio with a dividend yield of 4% should do the job. While at the same time preserving the shares that deliver this yield. However, it also needs to grow that income stream to keep pace with inflation every year. And that's the challenge. Some digitally savvy boomers stumbled across dividend-growth stocks en route to retirement. Some of these stocks have a yield of 4%, maybe more. And many of these companies increase that dividend every year. A retirement portfolio of such stocks could take care of the 4% Rule & inflation all at once. Boomers got interested. What might a portfolio of these dividend-growth stocks do for a younger investor?

This is a different approach to investing. Let's see how you think this approach compares to buying all the hot stocks your friends talk about over lunch.

3. How Much is Enough?

It's tough to imagine retirement when you're young. I know I couldn't see what was coming down the pike for me. I had decades left to fix things. I had way more exciting things to think about in my twenties & thirties. Even well into my forties. Retirement wasn't on my mind back then & no amount of advice from old people was going to change that. I wish someone had told me about financial freedom though.

What does financial freedom mean?

If you're happy on your current salary, you will achieve financial freedom when you have a portfolio capable of generating an income stream big enough to replace that salary. Once you have a portfolio that can deliver that, you never **need** to work again. You may choose to. But you don't **have** to. That's financial freedom. Look, if you think you need a little more than your current salary for comfort, then use that bigger number to figure out how big a portfolio you'll need. Just don't get too silly here! The important thing is that once you have a portfolio goal in mind, you can calculate what you need to save to get there. The savings rate is the bit you have most control over & that is the key thing to know as you set out on the path.

For example, let's say our hypothetical financial freedom chaser is making $70k a year. If we use the 4%

withdrawal guideline, that salary can be replaced by a portfolio with a value of $1.75 million. Gulp!

A thirty-year-old, starting out with a $10k investment, adding $10k every year, at the historical 10% rate of return, will take just under 30 years to hit that. Thirty years? Okay, starting out, I know I made it sound a bit like financial freedom was just around the corner for you & I apologise for that. But the reality is that it's better to get-rich-slow, than to not get rich at all.

Let's look at a couple with an annual household income of $100k. That income would work very well for them in retirement. But they will need a portfolio of $2.5 million to replace that kind of income. That's pretty challenging. However, they both work, so it's possible. On top of that, they intend to work 'til 65 & they expect to collect something close to full OAS & CPP when they retire. At today's rates, that would be something over $45k in guaranteed income. So they need their investment portfolio to make up the difference of $65k. Using the 4% guideline again, a portfolio of just over $1.6 million can provide the additional income of $65k. They have a lot of advantages over the single guy in the last example. They both work. They both save & invest. They have almost full OAS & CPP. And they plan on working all the way to 65. This lucky couple can get away with a smaller portfolio to create the retirement they want.

Everyone will be different. To calculate what you need, take a guess at what you'll get from CPP & OAS, &

subtract that from your goal retirement "salary". Then divide that remaining number by 4 & multiply the answer by 100. We're using the 4% rule here, remember. That result is the end portfolio value you might need to support that level of income. Some will ignore the CPP & OAS to create a more aggressive savings plan. If that works out, the government pensions will be bonus income when they retire. They'll have a bigger income in retirement than when they worked. That'd be pretty awesome, eh!

Now real life is often very different to the simple examples above. Those target portfolio numbers are **much** higher than the savings of the average Canadian going into retirement today. And that's because most of us older folk didn't start saving & investing early enough. I'm hoping you will get on it early & do a better job.

But how do you get there from here?

Once you calculate your goal retirement income, plug your current savings numbers into a compound growth calculator & see if you can hit that number at your current rate of savings. If not, consider increasing your savings rate. If it looks like you'll do better than your target, stick with your current savings plan anyway. Overshooting is better than undershooting in this game. Go at it harder while you are young. You have time on your side. And who knows what challenges you'll face along the way. Lousy market returns, job loss, unplanned car replacements, the roof leaks, OMG it's twins, & who knows what else. There will always be some unexpected costs & financial potholes along the way. You might have some lucky bounces along the way too, but it's better to get ahead of the game sooner. This is where short-term goals come into play. If you're okay with $1,250,000.00 as your long-term target, then getting about $45k invested in the market by age 30 could get you all the way there. You'd never have to save another penny to hit your long-term target. Now, rather than 10%, if the market only delivers a 5% return over the course of your investing lifetime, you'd need to have $230k invested by age 30. That's a bigger challenge, so you'll need to save more, & for a longer period of time. This planning-for-the-future stuff is tough. But saving more, earlier, & over more years, will improve your chances for success.

I realise this is all very simplistic. Financial planners would fall off their chairs laughing. But it gives you a quick way to define both long-term portfolio targets, tomorrow's dream, & short-term savings goals, today's reality. You can build a workable savings plan around the short-term savings goals. And that's what we're trying to kick-start here. Your savings rate is the only thing you control.

About half of Canadian pre-retirees don't even know if they have enough savings for retirement. Almost one third of Canadians have **nothing** saved for retirement. This is not where you want to find yourself as you get closer to retiring. Of course, things will probably change over time & you can revise your targets accordingly. Saving more when necessary. Or backing off saving when not. Or when you just can't afford to save. But setting savings targets that you can work with, right away, should be one of the first steps on your plan.

We'll talk more about the FIRE (Financial Independence, Retire Early) movement later, but we'll stick with a regular retirement philosophy for the rest of this stock picking exercise.

4. Boomer Secret

I know you're getting impatient with me now, so let's whip the sheet off the stuff old people buy. The chart below compares the performance of some of Canada's well-known companies against the S&P 500 Index®. Before looking at the chart, some investors would think this a very boring selection of stocks. I used an index-tracker, the SPDR S&P 500® ETF Trust, ticker SPY, managed by State Street Global Advisors (SSGA) in the USA, for the comparison. The end value of SPY, in Canadian dollars, might be about 25% higher than the chart shows. I used SPY because the Canadian-listed ETFs haven't been around long enough to do the comparison over this timeline.

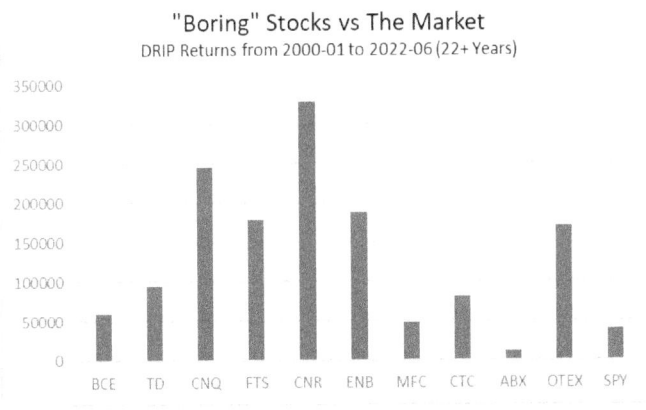

Fig. 4.4.1 Boring Stocks vs SPY® (22.5 years)

The columns show the end value of an original $10k

investment, with dividends reinvested for all equities, after twenty-two & a half years. The winning performance over this time, from CN Rail (CNR), turned 10k into almost $330k. A bank, a telco, an energy company, a tech business, a utility company & one of Canada's favourite tire stores all beat the big American index by a significant margin. The index return was just under $40k over this time. Or about $50k in Canadian dollars. Tell me you are not totally gobsmacked by the huge performance of some of these companies!

Look, I'm even more gobsmacked than you. I never saw the growth potential for companies like these. I had no idea of the true value of time. I knew nothing about dividends. And I had no idea of the added compounding power of dividend reinvestment. There are Dividend Reinvestment Plans (DRIP) offered directly by some companies, but many investors choose to DRIP through an online brokerage account. While you can't buy fractional shares at many brokerages yet, the dividends received will purchase the maximum whole number of shares covered by the dividend payment. Any leftover cash sits in the account 'til it gets combined with new money & invested later. There is no trading commission for DRIP share purchases with most brokerages & that is very important. The returns on these small dividend reinvestments would get hammered by a trading commission fee. Once you set it up, it's a very simple & automated process. The company pays a dividend, the brokerage reinvests the dividend in more shares of the same company for you. Automatically.

Buying boring stocks looks pretty interesting now, eh? But please don't rush off & start buying shares in any of these companies right away. There is more to this story, as you'll see. But first I'm going to tell you why retirees are interested in this approach. Then we'll consider how your goals might align with those of an older investor. Hang in there.

Note
I can't guarantee the precision of the above chart, nor that of a few others I'll share in the coming pages. I used several sources to gather data from & I may not have translated the comparison data perfectly. Validate the data yourself.

5. Retirement Goals

Going into retirement, some old codgers will be crying about having to sell the yacht & give up riding on the company jet. Many will be happy if they can afford a couple of winter breaks to the Caribbean. Others will be grateful if they can pay the rent & put food on the table. Sadly, there will be those who will struggle with doing that.

It's a long way off for you guys, but this is serious. And you need to know why you need to bother with all this saving & investing stuff so young.

In Canada, Canada Pension Plan (CPP) & Old Age Security (OAS) provide a baseline income for retirement. That won't be enough for a comfortable retirement. If you don't have a work pension, or some other source of income, your investment returns must provide for anything else you need. Like food! Generally, older folk worry about the safety of their investments & the income that comes from their portfolio. These are the primary drivers for increasing bond holdings with age. In the past, bonds have proven safer than stocks. Bonds produce a fixed income stream. But bond income has been trending lower over the past several decades, forcing older investors to explore alternatives. Dividend stocks, particularly dividend-growth stocks, are proving more popular these days. For investors, old & young. A key part of many retirement strategies now is to build a portfolio with a growing, rather than a fixed, income stream. Many retirees will not be adding new money to their accounts after retirement, so any growth in income must come from their investment choices. Dividend-growth investing can be part of the solution for them.

Does that strategy work?

With a portfolio allocation to dividend-growth stocks, it might. Here we will focus on Canadian dividend-growth stocks for the most part. Canadian companies are more biased towards paying higher dividends than American companies. You see that in the yield differences between the Canadian & American market index trackers. And, for those of us living in Canada, there are Canadian dividend tax advantages. Don't get me wrong here, the US is a fantastic market for dividend-growth stocks. But the yields are generally lower. And there are those potential US tax complications & the currency conversion costs to consider. Though some snowbirds like American dividends to cover their spending money when they head to Florida for winter.

For a retiree planning to live off interest, dividends & distributions, a good Canadian dividend income stream can be part of the solution. With a market index fund approach, the yields can be too low for the average portfolio to generate enough income to live on. With index ETFs, retirement income is generated by a combination of the low dividend payout & by selling some shares every year. Many retirees would rather **not** have to sell shares for living expenses. It can be tough to switch to selling, after a lifetime of buying. And there is fear of having to sell shares in a down market. That's why higher dividend yielding stocks have great appeal for retirees.

Let me be real here, this dividend-growth strategy is not trying to beat the market. While possible in theory, a selection of dividend stocks pulled together by the average investor in not likely to beat the index. Particularly if the selections are biased more towards the higher yielding companies. The total return from a portfolio of index ETFs will likely be better over time. But the **_psychological return_** from dividend-paying & dividend-growing companies suits the needs of some investors better. Dividend investors tend to focus on the dividends & not on the share price. So long as the dividends continue to flow & grow, dividend-growth investors tend to worry less about the share price fluctuations.

While those challenges are way down the road for you, we are going to explore the value of a dividend-growth strategy for a younger investor today. On the comparison chart, you saw the winning returns of some boring blue-chip stocks over the past 22 years. Those results show that it might work at both ends of the age spectrum. To be perfectly honest, had I adopted this old person's strategy back when I was your age, I might be retired already.

Let's see if it can work that way for you.

6. Picking the Right Growth Stocks

During strong bull markets, the upward trend of the indices is often powered by growth stocks. You'd think it would be easy to pick out the good growth stocks ahead of time. All you've got to do is buy the stocks that are powering the index, right? I have never been able to do that. Nor, it appears, can most professional money managers. Since most of them fail to beat the index most of the time, it must not be an easy thing to do. Even if you pick a few good growth stocks along the way, be wary of falling into the trap of believing that you can do it consistently. Everyone is a great stock picker in a raging bull market. Those high growth stocks can fall hardest during subsequent downturns.

Remember our chart of the boring stocks that beat the index? Over that same twenty-two & a half year timeframe, several well-known American companies would have beaten all of them. Apple (AAPL), for example, would have destroyed index returns with its end value of over 1.7 million dollars for that $10k investment. But nobody wanted Apple stock back in the early 2000s. Later, when things improved, I kept wanting to buy Apple. But I just couldn't see how it could grow much more. Wasn't it just a fad? Then, when it was no longer a fad, it seemed to be so overvalued that I never bought in. Silly me. Now Apple pays a dividend!

There is no question, if you can pick the right growth stocks, you will kill it. Nothing else compares. I could never figure out how to pick the right growth stocks. But the S&P 500® index has great growth potential too. A low-cost, index-tracking fund is a great core holding for long-term growth.

So that I don't leave you with the impression that any old Canadian blue-chip stock will trounce the market regularly, let me share another couple of charts that will give you a slightly different perspective from the earlier one.

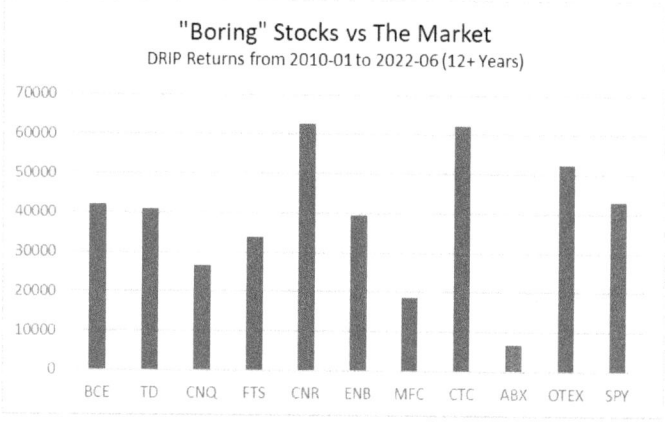

Fig. 4.6.1 Boring Stocks vs SPY® (Past 12.5 Years)

This chart has the same stocks as the previous one, but it covers the performance over the past 12.5 years. Only three of the ten beat the US index over this timespan. Only two when adjusted for currency. The rest have fallen behind market returns. To be fair, it's not too shabby a performance for most of them either. But the comparison over this more recent & shorter time span changes how things look, compared to the huge market-beating performance in the earlier chart. I chose these companies to show what is possible, but there were losers on the Canadian market over that timeframe too. Picking a portfolio of the wrong stocks could easily have produced a far poorer outcome. Given its greater diversity & overall solid performance, the index is starting to look better now.

Here is a more recent view of those same stocks, but now we're just looking back 5.5 years. In this chart, only one is outperforming the index. None when we consider the currency exchange rate.

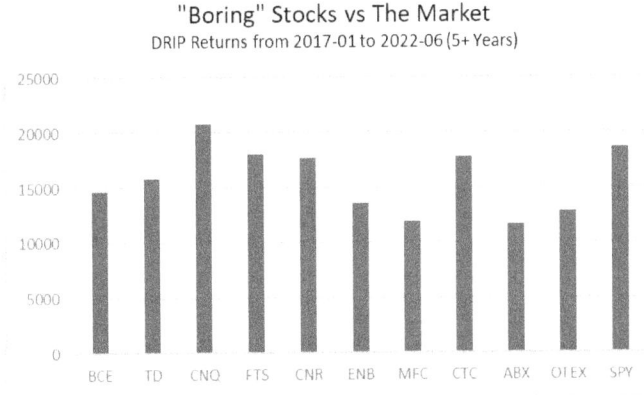

Fig. 4.6.2 Boring Stocks vs SPY® (Past 5.5 Years)

An energy stock, Canadian Natural Resources (CNQ), came from behind & leads the stock pack in this one. The rapid rise in the price of the oil during the covid pandemic, & the conflict in eastern Europe, drove the good results for energy stocks over recent years. It's important to review comparison charts over different time spans. Charts are historical, not prophetic. But trends change over time & it can be insightful to see how things changed in the past. If we could predict the trends accurately, we might be able to beat the market. But who can do that?

The big contribution to the performance problem for the index in the twenty-two & a half year chart was the inclusion of the "lost decade", from about 2000 to 2010. This included the bursting of the dot-com bubble in 2000 & the financial crisis of 2008. The Canadian market fared better than the American market during that decade. As did the Canadian stocks in the charts. That's the way investing is, things change. And it's impossible to forecast how things will change in the future.

If you want to buy individual growth stocks, the big question is this: can you pick the *next* Alphabet (Google), Apple, or Amazon? There are hundreds, thousands, of contenders out there. If you can't, index investing will at least ensure that you have all the big winners in your basket. If I had it to do over again, I would stick with index investing. Though I would also diversify beyond the US market. In this example, I compared Canadian stocks against an American index. Only because the American index is the most widely used for performance benchmarking. Try it yourself against the Canadian index.

Comparing these Canadian blue-chip stocks to the index isn't only about returns though. There are other factors worth considering.

I can get very emotional about my money. How about you?

7. Emotional Investing

Investing can be an emotional process. Most of us feel & fear loss to a far greater extent than we feel, or take pleasure in, an equivalent gain. Finding a $100 bill is a bit of a buzz. But, by comparison, losing a $100 bill is devastating. The fear in investing is often tied to the fear of loss. I've had some experience with losses. I remember them all too well. In later years, when I was buying dividend growth stocks, I tended to worry less. Because I was focused on the dividend stream & on reinvesting those dividends. Not on the share price. Dividends seem to make the share price matter less. Though I admit, I still looked at the share price too. This is even more important for a retiree.

A retiree who is all in on a low-yielding, index-tracking funds sells some shares every year for income. If the market tanks by 50%, our retiree will need to sell twice as many shares for the same income. Just thinking about that makes me feel ill. Mathematically, everything might continue to work for the index over a longer horizon. But the short-term downturns are very difficult to handle if you need to sell shares. It would be nice if a retirement portfolio was generating sufficient dividend income to live on, **without** the need to sell **any** shares. Moreover, we want to see that income stream grow every year. Ideally by at least as much as inflation. A dividend income stream from profitable, dividend-growth companies might be able to do that. And if the rate of dividend growth can outpace inflation, that might avoid the need to ever sell shares. Even during a year when the market is down.

What happens to dividends when the market goes down?

Here again, blue-chip dividend growers show some resilience. Many of these companies can sustain dividends during market downturns. Some may even continue to increase them. When share prices drop, a quality dividend income stream is more likely to hold up. When a growth stock goes down, there's nothing to look at but the declining share price. Mathematically, logically, historically, the market index may provide greater total returns. But emotionally, many investors are all over the dividend income stream instead. They are willing to sacrifice some of the potential market return for that added peace of mind. For a retired investor, dividend growth stocks might be a better way to get a good night's sleep. And that is an emotional investing decision that some investors find easy to make.

How might this work for a younger investor?

Young & growing companies like to reinvest all their profits (assuming they have profits!) in growing the business. Therefore, no dividends go out to shareholders. The value of the shares of a growth company is based on that strong growth outlook holding up well into the future. More mature companies tend to have less opportunity to reinvest their profits for such dramatic growth. These mature businesses are more likely to share some of their profits with shareholders, as dividends. But that does not mean they have zero growth. Only those that continue to grow earnings & profits can reliably increase dividends to shareholders. If a company is wisely investing some of its capital for profitable growth, & sharing the rest as dividends, what do you think that does to their share price?

Imagine buying a share of a company ten years ago for $100. It was paying a 5% dividend, or $5 per share. If that company increased its dividend every year since then, what do you think a new investor would be willing to pay for a share of that same company today? Assuming they maintained the same 5% dividend yield.

Let's say our company grew the dividend every year for those 10 years & you were getting $8.95 for every share today. You'd be pretty pleased, that's an annual dividend-growth rate of 6% since you bought in. Today, new investors would still be happy to buy a share of that same stock with a 5% yield. But $8.95 is a 5% yield on a share price of $179.00. A dividend-growth company can gradually increase the value of each share, possibly with less volatility, while paying an ever-increasing dividend along the way. The investor benefits from dividend growth **and** share price appreciation. That's not a bad way to build wealth.

During the accumulation years, those dividends are reinvested back into more shares of the same company. Those new shares pay even more dividend dollars. And all those dividends will buy an even greater number of shares during market downturns, when the share price is lower. This is like adding an automatic savings plan to a portfolio. And it's part of the compounding growth process for a dividend-growth investor. Dividend reinvestment, doing the DRIP, is like giving vitamins to a portfolio.

The growth argument against this is that the growth company is doing the reinvesting, more tax efficiently, on behalf of shareholders. And is therefore providing still greater growth potential. That's true. But then I'm back to trying to figure out which growth company does that well. Some investors would rather have the money in their hands. Then they can decide what to invest it in. Or they can choose to use it for income during retirement.

One of the reasons that good dividend-paying companies can be more resilient in a downturn is because of that relationship between share price & dividend yield. Imagine our $100 a share company is paying that $5 dividend annually. When the market crashes & the share price suddenly drops to $80, that $5 dividend is now a yield of 6.25%. If the company's business outlook remains solid during the downturn, & if the dividend continues to be considered safe, money will start to flow into that stock because of the higher yield percentage. You'll hear experts tout investing in strong dividend stocks as being "paid to wait" in a down or sideways market. In other words, while the market is declining or doing nothing, a dividend stock is still throwing cash to the shareholder. This tends to put the brakes on the falling share price of a dividend-paying company. Professional portfolio managers might even be selling some of their falling growth stocks & putting the money into some of these now-on-sale dividend paying companies instead. Along with the potential for decent returns, a diversified portfolio of dividend-growth companies can be a little less volatile.

There are companies that do share buybacks instead of, or in addition to, paying dividends. A share buyback means the company buys shares back from the market &, therefore, the value of the remaining shares on the market goes up. The entire company is worth the same, before & after a buyback. But when there are fewer shares available to the market after a buyback, each remaining share is worth a little bit more. Opinions vary on which approach is best for the shareholder. I like both but from an emotional perspective, I prefer to see dividends rolling into my account. Buybacks are great too. But only if companies do buybacks that add shareholder value. Like when the share price is low & offers value. Companies that invest in their own shares need to invest wisely too.

We will look at the dividend-growth strategy in more detail but first, we need to understand the total return profile of a dividend stock. This is of huge importance when comparing companies that pay dividends against those that don't. Pay attention to this. I didn't get this soon enough. And not understanding this is what foolishly had me selling off my dividend-paying stocks in my early years of investing. Dividend paying stocks might not just be for old people.

8. Comparing Returns

It sounds like a bit of a yawn, but it's not. You need to *get* this right off the bat. So that you don't dismiss dividend-paying stocks too quickly. This is one of the areas of greatest confusion & misunderstanding for new investors. When using online charts for comparing the history of investments, you need to know exactly what you are looking at. We're talking history here, so don't assume that what's happened in the past will happen in the future. But you do need to understand the type of return history you are looking at. Make sure you understand how to compare returns.

There are two types of return that you'll find being discussed & used for comparison purposes. The most commonly used charts online show **share price return**. That is exactly what it sounds like: the stock chart shows the share price performance over time. These charts do *not* consider any dividends or distributions that were paid to shareholders. They do *not* consider dividend reinvestment. Most of the online charts can handle more than one stock or ETF, so you can compare the relative performance of two or more over time. Here, the charts of growth stocks can look fantastic when compared to the share price appreciation of dividend-paying stocks. In part, this is because the dividends from these stocks don't appear on the chart. Share price returns are shown on the stock charts at sites like Google Finance & Yahoo Finance.

A better level of insight comes from **total return** charts. The total return of an investment is the share price return *with* all dividends & distributions reinvested in more shares of the same company or ETF. With total return charts, you get a true picture of the performance of a dividend-paying company. A chart that shows this kind of return is the ideal way to compare dividend-paying stocks against growth stocks. Especially when you are accumulating & growing a portfolio. A total return chart shows what dividend reinvesting, or turning on the DRIP, is all about. Reinvested dividends can really juice the total return. Especially when the company is consistently growing its dividend payout.

DRIP Return Charts Online
The Dividend Channel (dividendchannel.com) has a DRIP Returns Calculator that allows for comparison of two equities. It produces a nice set of charts & data that show the results with & without dividends reinvested. You can also find total return charts at stockcharts.com, under the PerfChart® link. Here, you can compare up to 10 ticker symbols. The default chart is a total return chart, but you can compare the same stock or ETF against itself, with & without dividends reinvested. Put an underscore before the ticker symbol for the share-price-only return chart. This makes for an eye-popping comparison on the power of dividends over time.

One of the most powerful tools for this kind of comparison is at the Portfolio Visualizer website (portfoliovisualizer.com). Use their "Backtest Portfolio" tool. Here, you can set up one stock in each of three available portfolios. Make each stock or ETF 100% of each portfolio & toggle the "Reinvest Dividends" line to "Yes". Now you're looking at the true total return power of a dividend stock, with those dividends reinvested. Toggle the "Display Income" setting to "Yes" & you'll see the historical annual income that was generated & reinvested. When the "Reinvest Dividends" field is toggled to "No", you'll see a couple of things of great interest to retirees & FIRE aficionados. The first is the income stream, right at the bottom of the Summary page. You can also now see if both the stock price **and** the income stream have a history of growth, but **without** dividends being reinvested. This is very important for checking the potential growth of an income stream that you plan to live on during retirement. The free tools at all these sites are a great resource for the DIY investor. Don't be surprised if you find yourself signing up for the paid version as your portfolio grows.

As we saw in the Boomer Secret chapter, those Canadian large cap companies, with dividends reinvested, fared better than the market index funds over that twenty-two & a half year timeframe. Large, stable, dividend-growth companies, profitably growing their business over time, could be good choices for your first few stocks.

You should spend time learning & using all these comparison & analysis tools. Watch the training videos on these websites, read the instructions. The more you play with them, the more features you will uncover. These tools can add value to your assessment process. Try them with a variety of stocks & ETFs. When you compare different types of investment using these tools, you will have a better understanding of the true nature of their returns. While past performance is no guarantee of future results, some investors prefer to own something with a good history of share price appreciation **and** dividend growth. Over a stock or a fund with an income stream that declines over time when dividend reinvestment stops.

Take the time to understand returns & how the information is presented. It is important for comparing stocks, ETFs, & your own portfolio.

9. Stock Selection

In the same way that you need a system to make saving a regular habit. You need a system to follow when it comes to investing. It can be as simple as just buying more shares of an index-tracking ETF with a portion of every paycheque. That is totally fine. It gets a little more complex when it comes to making individual stock selections. It's useful, maybe even necessary, to have an appropriate technical education to choose stocks with a greater probability of getting a good result. It's not that professionals can pick all winners, all the time. They can't. But perhaps they can avoid losers better than the uneducated. Since I don't have that education, I can't, for the life of me, figure out a way to buy growth stocks. But it feels a little easier to find decent dividend-growth stocks. Notice I said "feels" there? Not very technical, eh!

While the primary goal of the retiree is to build a more stable income stream, dividend-growth stocks have the potential for decent share price appreciation too. In fact, dividends have contributed a good portion of the overall return of the market indices throughout the history of stock markets. Dividend-growth stocks offer the potential for both income growth ***and*** share price appreciation. Moreover, they may provide that growth with a little less volatility & with less exposure to sequence of returns risk for those going into retirement.

Just looking at the numbers, we don't really care where the returns come from. But with a pure growth stock, we are exposed to greater sequence of returns risk in retirement. What's that? Imagine someone retires & the market crashes. It continues to decline for the first few years of retirement. Our retiree is forced to sell more shares of a declining portfolio to generate enough income to live on. Every share sold is like selling a goose from a flock that lays golden eggs. That impacts the income potential for the rest of the life of that portfolio & for that person. A retiree living off dividends might be able to avoid some of the sequence risk. Since fewer or no shares are sold during the downturn. That's a big deal. And that's why retirees consider a portfolio of dividend paying stocks worthwhile.

Let's look at an example of a shortlisting & screening process for stocks that might be considered for the dividend-growth part of a portfolio. This is **not** a definitive guide to stock picking. Rather, it is an example that illustrates how much extra work you need to put into stock picking. If you're new to investing, this will hurt your head! It might even scare you into investing in index-tracking ETFs at a young enough age that you might never have to bother with stock picking.

This is a sample screening process for illustration purposes only. Do not blindly jump into the market with this as your selection process.

Shortlisting & Screening Process

Investors closer to retirement might choose stocks that offer …

1. Dividend yields of 3% or greater
2. Dividend growth history of 10 years or longer
3. Without a sharply declining dividend growth trend or token dividend increases to maintain dividend growth status
4. Average 5-year dividend growth rate of 4% or more (average inflation is about 2.5%)
5. A current dividend yield that is higher than the average dividend yield for the past 5 years
6. Compares well to peers for value
7. Recommended by analysts or professional money managers

This a baseline screening process, a more rigorous evaluation process is required before pulling the trigger on any stocks that make it through. The dividend growth rate is very important. Remember, the dividend growth rate percentage is *not* the dividend yield. It is the rate at which the dividend income increases, year over year, as a dividend-growth company increases its dividend. If the *dividend yield* on a portfolio is enough to supplement a retiree's pension upon retiring, then the *dividend growth rate* is what keeps that income stream ahead of inflation over the course of a long retirement. This is especially critical for anyone contemplating retiring at a young age. A portfolio with no additional investment, but with an average dividend growth rate of 6.5%, for example, means the dividend income stream doubles every 11 years. Without buying any additional shares. I know my day job paycheque hasn't doubled over the past 11 years! Of course, it may not work out perfectly every year, but the potential for income to stay ahead of inflation is built into a dividend-growth portfolio.

These screening guidelines are probably more suited to an older investor. A company paying a lower dividend, but with a higher dividend growth rate, could be a better choice for a young investor. High rates of dividend increase tend to back off over time. But there's nothing wrong with taking the oomph of a higher annual dividend increase while it's available. And before the company gets to that more mature & stable stage, when the dividend growth rate will taper off to a lower, hopefully still sustainable, level. A young investor has more time to work with, so a faster dividend grower might produce a better long-term result. Both for income growth & for share price appreciation. It is the combination of dividend yield & dividend growth rate that you need to look for. A stock with a lower dividend yield, but a higher dividend growth rate, can work well over time.

In retirement, the higher dividend yield becomes more important for an investor who wants to live off those dividends. Unfortunately, we can't just fill our portfolios with all the highest dividend yielders. There are unsafe limits of dividend payout. Dividends can be too high for some companies to sustain. Hunt around online & everyone has a different opinion. Don't go above 4%

yield, stay below 5%, & some say you'll commit investing suicide with a 6% yield. That's too general to be of much use. And dividends tend to be higher in Canada, compared to the US. An American investor might be horrified by some of the high dividend yields available with some Canadian companies. Yet, companies with higher dividend yields are cornerstones of many personally & professionally managed portfolios in Canada. Including many of the pension funds, ETFs & mutual funds that Canadians are invested in.

Just keep in mind that there is no perfect set of rules you can apply to evaluating a stock that tells you exactly what to buy, when to buy, & when to sell. There are no sets of numbers that guarantee a good outcome for an investment. While we can tilt the odds more in our favour, dividend-growth investing doesn't come with a crystal ball either.

Professionals look at current valuations, dividend payout ratios, free cash flow numbers, return on invested capital, shareholder return, & a bunch of other metrics that can be challenging for a DIY investor to interpret.

This is starting to sound like a lot of work, eh?

10. Stock Shortlisting Process

Okay, we've got a basic set of criteria for the kind of stocks we want in our dividend-growth portfolio, what now? Unfortunately, a lot more work. Start off with a list of the largest companies in Canada, you'll find plenty of lists online. Or you can use the holdings of ETFs like XIU or CDZ. Stick them all into a spreadsheet & sort them by dividend yield. Now lop off any below your dividend yield threshold. For this example, I would lop off any below 2%. Despite the first requirement being 3%, it's good to watch for opportunities outside the target limit. A sudden drop in the markets might boost a company's yield into acceptable territory. If a $100 stock yielding $2.80, or 2.8%, for example, suddenly falls to $80, that same $2.80 dividend immediately turns into a 3.5% yield. If the company & dividend outlooks remain healthy during the dip, that stock just went on sale & it now passes the minimum requirement for yield.

Sign up for a free account at Morningstar.ca & create a portfolio of all your shortlisted stocks. If the default view configuration doesn't already have it, add columns for the 1, 3 & 5-year dividend growth rates. It's a play portfolio, so play-buy $10k worth of each stock on your list. Divide 10,000 by the current share price to figure out how many shares you need to add. You can use fractional shares here, to more closely match the $10k allocation. Now let's compare an individual stock against the remainder of the selection criteria.

On Morningstar.ca, key in the ticker symbol in the "Search Quotes" box & select the stock you're looking at from the drop-down list. Make sure you get the Canadian-listed (TSE) version. Some Canadian companies are listed on both the Toronto Stock Exchange & on the New York Stock Exchange. Under the "Dividends" tab, you'll find most of the other info required for the process.

In the Dividends and Splits table, you'll see columns of info for 7 years, starting 10 years ago. You need to scroll right to see the most recent 3 years, along with some other info we need. The first row of data shows, in dollars & cents, the payout per share. To meet the 2nd requirement, that number needs to be increasing every year for the entire 10 years. The increases will vary in amount, so look for trends. Consistently declining increases are usually not a good sign. If the first 7 years show good increases & the final 3 years are showing small increases, that's a possible red flag. Those are some of the trends covered by the 3rd requirement. Let's assume we've got a good one & we can move on to the 4th requirement, the Average 5-Year Dividend Growth Rate. For this, we need to go to our new play portfolio & look at the data in the column under the 5-Year Dividend Growth Rate header. If it's more than our target, that's good. But you should also look at the 1- & 3-year dividend growth rates to see if the trend is downward in more recent history. A 10% rate over 5 years, combined with a 5% rate over 3, & only a 2% increase over 1 year might be a sign of trouble to come. Perhaps the dividend growth rate cannot be sustained. Something reasonably flat & consistent here might be fine. Some sectors, like utilities, tend to look less aggressive. But they have their place in a portfolio too. Let's assume we're still good with our current candidate, we can then go back to the Dividends tab & scroll all the way to the right. Here we compare the Current Trailing Dividend Yield % against the 5-Yr Average. If the current yield is higher than the historical average, that is an indication that the stock might be on sale. If the current yield is lower, that might mean that a lot of other investors saw the value & bid up the share price. It would be useful to calculate the 10-year average too. It's just a little extra work. This is the same idea as the example we looked at earlier, where the $100 stock was paying $5 for a 5% yield. If the share price drops to $80 as part of a broader market downturn, that $5 dividend is now a 6.25% yield. The higher yield percentage today, compared to the average 5% yield over the past 5 years, might mean the stock is on sale.

We're not done yet, but there are potential issues that can crop up with this process. When I looked at the Dividend Growth Rate columns today (March 2022), all the big Canadian banks pass the requirement for the 5-year dividend growth rate. But some show zero growth over the past year. Should we toss them out for not growing the dividend? Not in this case, as it happens. The Office of the Superintendent of Financial

Institutions (OSFI) is an independent government agency that tries to assure that our banking system is safe. They supervise & regulate our federally registered banks & insurers. During the pandemic, as a safety measure, OSFI saw fit to instruct these financial institutions to not raise their dividends. We are looking for dividend growers, but this external prevention of dividend growth would not stop me from owning a Canadian bank. There are exceptions to most rules! And this is another example of the added work required for stock picking. You needed to pay attention to the company & financial news to know that this was the case.

The 6th requirement requires us to do all the above, for all the contenders in a category. So, for example, if we were choosing our next big bank stock to buy, we should compare our choice with the rest of the big 6 banks. Since we all have different requirements, it will come as no surprise that 6 different investors might each come up with a different bank selection for their portfolio. A conservative investor might choose the largest bank, a young investor might choose the fastest growing bank, a more aggressive investor could go with the fastest dividend grower, a retiree might want the one with the biggest dividend, & so on. Most Canadian investors will have more than one bank in their portfolio, as do most Canadian focused ETFs. Morningstar does a great job of pulling all these data together for us, but you should always check the data on the investor's page of the company's website too.

Starting out, this is tough stuff to wade through, eh? What's worse is that this is just a shortlisting process, it's not a complete selection process. To do that well, we really should be able to read & understand financial statements. We should understand more about safe payout ratios, price to earnings multiples, return on invested capital, & a host of other financial measurements that could help us avoid investing mistakes. While some will embrace the challenge & enjoy the learning experience, others will run away screaming. Or we can outsource the tough stuff. For me, the 7th point is an acknowledgement of my own inability to do all that financial analysis well. I'm hoping someone else will do that for me.

That's the next chapter.

11. Lean on the Pros

Many of us cannot handle all that stock analysis stuff we covered in the last chapter. Instead, we lean on information from sources like the analytical reports that are included with our brokerage accounts. These provide analyst insights on the stock under consideration & comparisons with peer stocks. Most importantly, they provide a score across several metrics that can be used for comparison. In addition to using the brokerage resources, I have signed up for more than a few newsletters & financial advice services along the way. I think it's as difficult to pick a good newsletter as it is to pick a good stock. But since I cannot confidently rely on my own skills to assess a stock, I tend to rely on this 3rd party advice instead. The analysis of the business & the security of the dividend in these newsletters improves on my own very basic assessments. While I sometimes deviated from the newsletter guidelines, the advice gave me some additional comfort when deciding. And it occasionally stopped me choosing a total lemon.

I also record all the episodes of the Market Call® & Berman's Call® shows on BNN Bloomberg®. Since they do this on the shows, I feel obliged to say that BCE Inc. is the parent company of this network & I probably own shares of that company in one of my ETFs! On these shows, financial experts & money managers take viewers' calls on specific stocks. These are real money managers, taking care of real money, for real people. But this is TV, so this advice is **not** personalised for us, the viewer. In fact, the guests often mention that it is not investing advice. However, these professional opinions might corroborate, or not, my choices. I watch these shows as part of my regular routine. Though I try to do my own, admittedly very limited, due diligence, it does add to my knowledge & understanding. It can be reassuring to see these professional money managers recommend one of my stocks as one of their top picks. And I like it when they say they are adding new client money to one of my stocks. At least if I'm wrong, I won't be the only one losing money! These guests have repeat appearances so that, over time, you'll get to know them & their investing styles. It's important to understand the investing strategy of each guest. A quant trader may be buying a stock based on short term momentum. By the next appearance, this guest might have sold the recommended stock at a profit. We don't want to be left holding that same stock at a loss. Dividend-growth investing is a long-term, buy-and-hold strategy. The analysis provided by the guests who follow a similar approach to our chosen strategy is likely to be more useful. The more you watch, the better you will understand the strategies employed by the different professionals. During each show, the guest's past picks will be reviewed. From this, you will learn that even the pros can't pick winners all the time either. Just as with this book, use these shows for education &

entertainment purposes only, not for stock or ETF picking. For me, the tools & services included with my brokerage account are one of the best sources of information.

When I look at a potential investment in a particular sector, I also look around to see what its peers are doing. When choosing a big bank stock, compare it to the other banks. Due to my lack of an appropriate technical education, my comparisons are limited & basic. I might check the PE ratios of all six banks, for example, to see if my proposed purchase is in line with the rest of them. If it's totally out of whack, higher or lower, I'm forced to try & figure out why. Along with the Morningstar Financial Health Grade, there are several other ratios that you can add to your play portfolio at Morningstar.ca. Use these for quick comparisons to see if there are any red flags. For fun & the learning experience, build a couple of portfolios based on Morningstar's A & D rated stocks. Then, on Portfolio Visualizer, try back testing these portfolios to see how the returns compare. Did the "A"s do better than the "D"s? There are several other metrics that you can build into your process. Many of them can add further value to this simple screening process. I encourage you to learn more about the evaluation metrics used to assess the quality of a stock. Should you ever decide to go stock picking, I think the knowledge will serve you well.

Simple though this screening process is, it is incomplete & inadequate for stock selection. But it's an awful lot of work compared to just buying the same few ETFs over & over again, eh? And that's the whole point of putting you through this pain. Understand that stock picking takes a lot of work. Now, if you want to avoid all this work, start saving early & invest in your index ETFs. That approach might make you wealthy enough that you won't worry so much about dividend stocks come retirement day. You might find yourself in a position to swap your index ETFs for some dividend ETFs with a higher yield & just go enjoy yourself.

But if you still want to evaluate some stocks, or some different ETFs, we'll look at a complementary approach in the next chapter. This one takes a little learning too. But it's more about pictures than numbers.

That sounds way easier, eh!

12. Comparing Investments

Rather than put you through the agony of the previous chapters, I could have started with this. The reason I didn't is because it's too easy to believe that this comparison approach is the "solution" to stock picking. It's not. Humans are good with pictures & patterns. But when it comes to stocks, it's far too easy to reach the wrong conclusion by only looking at charts & graphs. Especially when the charts can only be about historical performance. Keep in mind that many failed companies once had charts that went up. Until they didn't! However, once you've done all the other work, there is value to comparing investment contenders with charts.

Along with Morningstar.ca, one of my favourite tools for reviewing past performance is Portfolio Visualizer. It is a fantastic tool for comparing stocks, to each other & to indices. It's great for comparing ETFs. Against each other & against stocks. You can compare entire portfolios of stocks & ETFs against other ETFs or a portfolios of ETFs. The charts of returns, with & without dividends reinvested, along with the income flows, can provide useful insights for retirement planning. It's a great tool for comparing different investing strategies too.

When comparing, do the exercise over differing time periods. Go back as far as the data will go. Then look at the past 15-, 10- & 5-year periods. This might highlight changing trends over different timelines. While the charts provide a visual representation, there are numbers for things like volatility & drawdowns too. This might help a more cautious investor choose a less volatile portfolio that won't bounce up & down as much as the markets. Look at the total return with dividends reinvested, & without. Look at the income stream with dividends reinvested, & without. In the Benchmark option, select "Specify Ticker" & use SPY or VFV.TO (shorter history) to compare the historical returns of your portfolio against those of the iconic US market index. You could use XIU.TO (portfoliovisualizer.com uses .TO extensions for Canadian-listed stocks & funds) if you want to compare your choices to the Canadian top 60 index. The beauty of Portfolio Visualizer is that it is not too challenging to get started with. Even the basic comparison charts will be useful. But the more you use these tools the more value you'll find in them. It's worth putting in the effort to learn. I know you'll be fascinated by the charts. Just don't fall into the trap of thinking that a picture is worth more that all that analysis we talked about earlier. And always remember that charts look backward, not forward. They are *not* crystal balls.

I chose to use dividend-growth stocks as an example of an investing strategy here. I think it is an easier strategy to learn. Done right, it can provide decent returns for investors young & old. And, depending on your choices, it may do that with less volatility than the market. But as good as it might sound, dividends aren't magically free money. Dividends are paid out of the company's after-tax profits. The value of the company goes down when the dividends go out. Had the company reinvested this money for new growth, that would be more efficient than us reinvesting those after-tax dividends back into the same company. Of course, not all companies striving for growth reinvest their profits wisely every time. But companies with a long & strong history of dividend payouts want to sustain that flow of cash to shareholders. Shareholders expect that. Now it's not like we're getting "free" money but, for many, it can be stress-free money. Dividends offer the potential to provide an income stream that does away with the need to sell shares. While dividend paying companies may not match a growth company's performance during a bull market, they may hold up a little better during a bear market. Buying dividend-growth companies tends to guide a portfolio a little more towards a quality & value style of investing. Though if we only consider dividend stocks, we are ruling out a large part of the diversity available in the total market. Since many companies don't pay dividends, we are missing out on exposure to what they might contribute. It is easy to make a case for using a broader selection process for diversity. Market index funds offer that greater diversity. But Canadians also need to add geographic & sector diversity by considering American & international exposure.

13. An American Income Stream

The requirements to qualify as a Dividend Aristocrat® in America are far more stringent than those in Canada. This list, & the associated indices created from it, is also managed by the S&P Global group that maintains the S&P 500® index. There are far more companies, with far longer histories of paying & growing dividends in the US. It is a bigger market for a dividend-growth investor. But it takes additional work, so it's not unusual to see Canadian investors sticking with ETFs for an American income stream. Same for international exposure.

There are several American-listed ETFs focused on dividend yield & growth. Check out US-listed ETFs like SCHD, NOBL, DGRO, VIG, VYM & HDV, for example. Look at the chart of the "Portfolio Income" on Portfolio Visualizer for those that provided a nice, generally upward, dividend-growth pattern over the past 10 years. I prefer to buy funds that have a 10-year history, or more. It's important to see how they perform during downturns. For the resilience of both the share price & the dividend stream. See if you can find the one that performs best. Then check the income stream, with & without dividends reinvested, to see if that shows an enduring growth trend. There are some decent choices here. The American market provides a lower yield than the Canadian market, but I think having American exposure is necessary, even for retirees. For the geographic & sector diversity it offers over the Canadian market.

Finding a Canadian-listed ETF filled with American dividend growers, one that offer increasing income year over year, is more of a challenge. But there are some that might work & they can be used for the American allocation in a Canadian investor's portfolio. In addition to ETFs like VFV, ZSP & XSP for market index tracking, look at BMO's ZDY & ZLU, Blackrock's XHU & XMU, & Vanguard Canada's VGG. These are more dividend biased or lower volatility solutions. Covered call ETFs offer greater income potential, usually by sacrificing some of the upside. Take a look at BMO's ZWH & Horizon's USCC, by way of example. There are many others, from these & other fund providers. Practice hunting them down & comparing the relative performances. For share price appreciation, dividend payout consistency & growth, & so on. Dividend ETFs provide a potentially good path for those closer to retirement. But if you feel the need to test out your stock picking skills, try a play portfolio of some Canadian dividend-growth companies. It might be a good learning experience before you get to an age where it might matter.

You will find foreign, that is outside North America, ETFs from most fund providers for developed & emerging markets too. They also have a place in a well-diversified portfolio. It's starting to sound a bit like one of those global all-equity ETFs now, eh? Just with dividends!

14. Luck & Commodities

I have no idea how to invest in shares of highly cyclical companies. Instead of trying to figure out how to pick the right commodity stocks at the wrong part of the cycle, I tried to time the market!

I know, I know! I said this is something we should never try to do. And we shouldn't. But when it comes to these kinds of stocks, I just can't figure out any other way to do it. I do not want to get into the trading game of trying to buy highly cyclical stocks at the lows & sell them at the highs. I want to buy shares in a good company, at a good price, & then go drink coffee. For the rest of my life. As it happens, that's one of my favourite commodities! Outside of the annual portfolio review, I really don't want to think about when I should sell a stock. Ideally, I never want to sell anything I own. I always seem to make a mess when I do.

My approach to buying these more volatile stocks was not very logical. I would identify a few big, blue-chip stocks that I liked in the space. And then wait for a disaster. Which can take years. And I wasn't always patient enough. Then, when the opportunities came along, I didn't always recognise them. Even when I did, I was usually too scared to take a full position & I tentatively, hesitantly, almost reluctantly, bought a small position. The covid crash was a perfect example. Canadian Natural Resources (CNQ) & Suncor (SU), two of Canada's largest energy companies, presented a great buying opportunity at that time. Though SU cut the dividend & went even lower after doing that, that only proved an even better buying opportunity. But who could have seen that coming? It's not just about oil. Nutrien (NTR), a company focused on the agricultural space, went low during this time too. It's tough to buy when everyone is scared & in panic mode. I scare easily too, so this is a very hit & miss approach. But I can't come up with any better way to buy these highly cyclical stocks than to tentatively dip my toe in when it looks like a totally insane time to do that. I strongly suggest that you find a better way.

Fast forward two & a half years from the covid crash & the companies mentioned above have performed really well. All are paying a nice & growing dividend. In the first half of 2022, the market was in turmoil because of ongoing covid challenges, supply chain issues, the war in Ukraine, rising interest rates & high inflation. These stocks did well & helped offset some of the losses being experienced by the markets at large. That's what diversification is all about & that's why it's useful to have some of these stocks in a portfolio.

Or maybe just stick with a low-cost index ETF that already holds them!

15. Portfolio Review

You should review your portfolio on a regular schedule. An important purpose of a portfolio review is to rebalance allocations. Though I sometimes try to avoid the work of rebalancing, it's the right thing to do. Another review requirement is to sell holdings that no longer meet the investment thesis or objective. I'm torn by this requirement too. I should, for example, sell shares of a company that no longer grows the dividend. And if there's a cut, it should be tossed. But then I remember the Coffee Can portfolio outcome & I don't want to rebalance & I don't want to sell the dogs!

This is a common dilemma for many DIY investors. We sometimes don't follow our own rules. I struggle to sell losers, hoping they'll at least get back to break even before I'm forced to sell. I worry about keeping the big winners. In fear of them going back down again. Next week I can feel exactly the opposite & I'll want to dump the losers & buy more of the winners. That's why we need a well-defined process. After years of doing this, I struggle to follow my own process sometimes. But the review process is probably more important when we hold individual stocks. As investors, we should review each holding using the same guidelines that were used for choosing the stock in the first place. Opinions vary on frequency, but I didn't want to do this more than once a year. I reviewed my portfolio sometime in

January. I'm sure there are better times of the year to do a review, particularly for a more active investor who is tax loss harvesting (looking for capital losses to offset against capital gains) in a taxable account, ahead of year end. But January was when I finalised all my spreadsheets for the previous year & my spreadsheets were more about the income. I wanted to see my total dividend income for the past year & I enjoyed comparing that number to the prior year's income. That's the fun side of dividend-growth investing … getting a pay raise!

Some investors are influenced by a "feel good" metric, Yield on Cost. Yield on Cost is exactly what is says: you calculate the yield based on the current dividend amount paid, against what the stock was originally purchased for. A stock bought for $100 paying a $5 dividend was an original 5% yield. If the dividend grows to $10, it might still only be a 5% yield on a $200 share price today, but that's a 10% yield on cost. Warren Buffett's yield on cost for his Coca-Cola (KO) shares is over 54% now. In other words, his annual dividend payment is worth more than half what he originally paid for all the shares way back when. And it gets bigger with each passing year. For long-time holdings, the Yield on Cost can be dramatic. But it's totally meaningless from an income perspective. If you sell those shares today & buy them back tomorrow for the same price, the new Yield on Cost drops to whatever the current dividend yield is. But you still get the same $10 payout. Exactly the same as when the Yield on Cost was through the roof. Yield on Cost does nothing for the size of the current income stream, but it still feels good. And while I guess there's nothing wrong with feeling good, don't hang on to investments with a high yield on cost number if they wouldn't meet your requirements for a buy today. Aside from potential capital gains exposure in a taxable account, it shouldn't be a consideration during review time.

The bottom line here is that the portfolio review is important, particularly when working with individual stocks. Or with multiple ETFs that need you need to rebalance yourself. It works best when you do it under a set of rules. There is little or no work to do when you hold ETFs that are rebalanced by the professional fund or index managers.

16. FIRE on High Yield

The Financial Independence Retire Early (FIRE) movement is more popular than ever & why wouldn't it be. It is financial freedom, only sooner. We've already seen the potential for dividend growth stocks & ETFs to provide income support for a lengthy retirement. But that's not the only route. Some FIRE folk favour high yield funds. This approach can deliver a bigger income stream, from a smaller portfolio. That could lead to retirement earlier than a traditional portfolio might allow. We've already talked about the psychological advantages of a divided-growth portfolio, so it's easy to transfer that kind of thinking across to funds that offer an even higher yield. We're focused on the yield not the share price, the income stream is automated, no need to sell shares, & so on. You can see the similarities. And the bonus is that many of these high yield funds come with yields of 10%, 15%, & sometimes more. If you need an income stream of $50k a year to retire on, a $500k dividend portfolio with a 4% yield only delivers $20k a year. Flip that portfolio over to funds with a 10% yield & you've hit your $50k income target right away.
Job done ... retire, eh?

FIRE has some additional challenges over the more traditional retirement age. Very early retirement means that CPP contributions stop early. That can eliminate a chunk of guaranteed index-linked retirement income.

The value of CPP should not be underestimated. This is the closest many of us will come to having some defined benefit pension income. That can be an important part of a retiree's long-term funding. Factor that into your planning for early retirement.

Just as with the dividend-growth approach, we should understand how these high-yield funds perform. We need to see if we get a reliable income stream, one that can keep pace with inflation, over the course of a longer retirement. To generate bigger yields, these funds use covered calls, leverage, split fund & other strategies. During the accumulation phase, with all those distributions reinvested, those funds can deliver a solid total return. There may be psychological & emotional returns with this investing approach too. While not all investors need to beat the market, any investing strategy must deliver an acceptable total return. We all have our own notion of what's acceptable. After retirement, we need to know that we have a portfolio capable of delivering a reliable income stream. One that can stay ahead of inflation. And for the remainder of our lives. Many of the same comparisons we did for the dividend-growth strategy apply here too. As do many of the warnings. We can't go & blindly buy the biggest yielding fund on the market & pray that it holds up. We need to evaluate the performance for the accumulation & decumulation phases, from both total return & income perspectives. We can use the same comparison tools as before to look at an example of what this might mean. I'm cherry-picking some investments here to illustrate a couple of points, but this example shows how important is it to understand how your choices can impact your retirement dreams.

The following chart shows the income stream from an American closed end fund ("CEF" is for convenience, that's not a ticker symbol), a popular Canadian income fund, & one of the big banks in Canada. I kept the tickers anonymous because you should learn to do this work yourself, with whatever funds you are considering. This selection is designed to highlight some of the potential pitfalls.

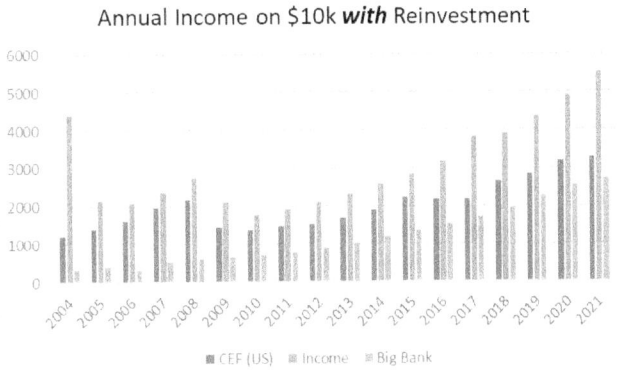

4.16.1 Annual Income on $10k with all distributions reinvested.

The income streams from both high-yield funds are significantly higher than that of the bank. Despite the bank's dividend income showing a consistent growth pattern, the income streams from the two funds are still crushing the bank after 18 years. This is looking pretty good for the funds over the dividend-growth stock, eh?

However, this chart only considers the distributions. When we look at the total return for each, with all distributions reinvested, we get the true accumulation picture. I added the index for comparison.

With Reinvestment (2004 - 2021)				
	CEF (US)	Income	Big Bank	Index
CAGR	5.5%	10.9%	12.7%	10.5%

The closed end fund had the highest yield but, despite reinvesting all those big distributions, it provided the lowest total return. The Canadian income fund did a great job, even beating the American index in the process. While the big bank used in this example beat them all. The lesson here is that high yields do not always make for the best total return. Even when all the dividends & distributions are reinvested. Though you can find some high-income funds that do a good job, be sure to look at the total return picture of any fund you plan to use during the accumulation years.

Here's another way to look at this ...
With all dividends & distributions reinvested, the closed end fund would have turned US$10k into almost US$26.5k ($33.5k Canadian) by the end of 2021. The bank would have turned $10k into more than $85k. An investor who planned on retiring at the end of 2021 could sell the bank on retirement day & buy a fund with a far bigger income stream! The Canadian income fund

finished 2021 over $64k in value & the index over US$60k, or almost $76k Canadian.

Next, we'll look at the income stream of each, with DRIP off. In retirement, the dividends & distributions from these investments will replace the income from a day job. They will no longer be reinvested.

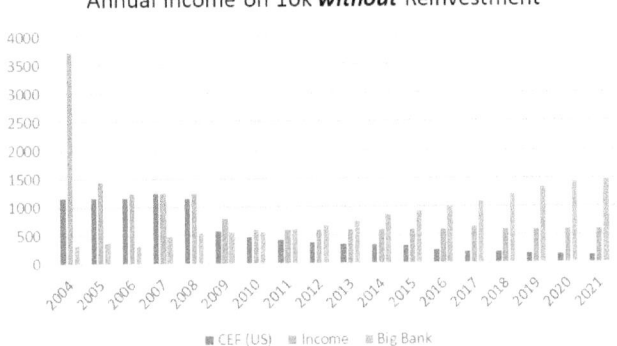

Annual Income on 10k **without** Reinvestment

4.16.2 Annual Income on $10k with all distributions NOT reinvested.

Now it gets interesting! This chart shows the income stream from the same three investments but, this time, it's for investors who retired in 2004 & took out all the dividends & distributions every year. While those big payouts from the high yield funds look great in the early years of retirement, it won't feel so great watching the income stream decline as time goes by. When we combine a declining annual income with inflation, retirement will get more challenging with each passing year. Though the early years look great, the closed end fund is the poorest result here. Income is consistently going down. The Canadian income fund, on the other hand, looks stable over the last dozen years. That's a good performance. But for long-term retirement income, the winner is the bank. It has grown the income stream in almost every year. Imagine a 40-year-old taking early retirement in 2004. After 18 years of enjoying the good life, our FIRE retiree is still a couple of years away from collecting a (greatly reduced) CPP pension, & OAS. The total income, adding all the dividends & distributions from every year, delivered by the closed end fund up to the end of October 2022, was just short of $12k ($15k Canadian). The Canadian income fund distributions totalled just over $17k. While the bank paid out just over $16k. Going forward, if the bank continues to increase its dividend, it will likely outperform the total income delivered by either high-yield fund. In this example, the bank looks like a better option for long-term, inflation-beating income.

Unfortunately, things only get worse from here. If we look at the growth rate of the underlying investments, without the dividends & distributions reinvested over those 18 years, it looks like this ...

Without Reinvestment (2004 - 2021)				
	CEF (US)	Income	Big Bank	Index
CAGR	-12.0%	-2.3%	8.7%	8.4%

In addition to an increasingly impaired income stream, annualised returns are negative for the high yield funds. Both the income stream *and the share price* went down over this time. The bank shares are worth almost $45k at the end of 2021. The closed end fund shares are worth less than a thousand dollars. That will create some serious pain should a retiree ever need to sell shares to cover an unexpected emergency later in retirement. Reinvesting some of the distributions in the early years will delay some of the pain for the closed end fund. But the lower CAGR we saw with full reinvestment suggests that it was always a poorer proposition over that timeline. This shows how important the CAGR comparison is.

Now to be fair, the closed end fund may do better going forward, who knows. There are other high-yield funds out there with different return profiles, some look pretty good. You should evaluate several of these funds to ensure they meet your needs. And before you take on the risks of early retirement. Even this fund might suit some. An older retiree with a limited spending horizon, for example, might find the huge early income useful. A retiree with a plan to do a lot of travelling in the first 5 years of retirement might need greater cash flow only during those early years. If maintaining capital to leave an inheritance is of no importance, they could work for that kind of investor. But for those with a longer horizon, a fund that can preserve more of the share value & the income stream might be a better choice.

High yield has great appeal, it's a great way to generate a retirement "salary". Use the comparison tools & look at the history carefully. Be wary of oversimplify the math. Thinking that a 15% yield means the "cost" is "paid off" in under 7 years & that it's all "profit" after that sounds right. But these simple calculations can mask a downward trend in share value & payout dollars over time. Learn how to use the comparison tools to help assess the potential for building a retirement income stream that will survive longer than you will. Review the CAGR over different timelines. It might be worth favouring funds that have been around a while, so you can study the historical performance. Past performance is no guarantee for the future. But if I find a few funds that have proven they can maintain the income stream & the share price over time, I might add some to my own retirement portfolio for the go-go years! However, that doesn't mean that they are the best option for a younger investor. If you think the approach suits your investor psychology better, then check it out more thoroughly. But it might be challenged to beat the low-cost indexing strategy over a long enough time. And going the indexing route might mean you can buy that bigger income stream when you retire. Another call you'll have to make for yourself.

The bottom line is this ... if you find yourself enchanted by high yield funds, don't leap out of the frying pan & into the FIRE movement too early!

17. Sequence & Inflation Risk for FIRE

We touched on this for older retirees earlier, but sequence of returns risk may be an even bigger deal for younger retirees, since they have many more years of retirement to get through. Come retirement day, sequence of returns risk is a horror story waiting to happen. Retiring just ahead of a market crash, the decline in portfolio value means that taking out the planned 4% will hurt more. If there are a few bad years in a row, the problem gets worse. The portfolio shrinks faster than was planned. Selling more shares of a shrinking portfolio makes the fear of running out of money very real. This early damage can have a big impact on the rest of the life of the portfolio. As we saw in the last chapter, high yielding portfolios might not be the best long-term solution either. Could a dividend-growth portfolio provide a smoother glide path? Possibly. The yields will not match those available from high-yield funds, but the history of delivering income growth is good. Of course, that means you'll have to put off retirement for a few more years. You'll need a bigger portfolio to live off a 4% dividend yield. Some use a cash-bond-stock bucket approach to help mitigate sequence of returns risk. Spending the cash & using the bonds until the market recovers can help avoid selling beaten down shares.

Inflation can damage retirement portfolios too. We've had many years with an average inflation rate of about 2.5%. That rate of inflation is typically catered for in retirement planning. But what happens when inflation suddenly jumps to 6 or 8%, maybe more, shortly after retirement day? And if it remains high for the first 3 or 4 years of retirement? Inflation drives prices up. They rarely come back down. More shares of a growth or index portfolio need to be sold to maintain living standards. Can you imagine being hit with sequence of returns losses & inflation at the same time? A terrible scenario for new retirees.

If you managed to wade your way through all the stuff on stock picking, you can see that a dividend-growth portfolio can be part of the solution for sequence of returns & inflation problems for a younger retiree. The strategy has some potential to hold up during down markets, so that shares may not need to be sold. It may not keep pace with periodic high spikes in inflation, but a good dividend-growth portfolio might stay ahead of inflation over the long haul. And if shares must be sold, dividend paying stocks can hold up better during turbulent markets. Along with a cash & bond allocation in a bucket strategy, there may be some valid reasons to have part of a FIRE portfolio in good dividend-growth stocks or ETFs. But even with that, some retirees may need to be flexible with their income requirements when bad things happen to the markets.

Now, if you retire after a market crash & have some fantastic growth years immediately following your retirement, you might wind up getting very rich. Your children might never have to work. Start teaching your kids about all this early!

18. The Covid Conundrum

While FIRE has been around since well before the pandemic, interest in early retirement has skyrocketed since we were all forced to work from home. Some who can't even contemplate retirement yet don't want to go back to the office fulltime anymore. And why would we? It was great to be able spend time messing around on our laptops & devices during the lockdown period. Without having to keep an eye out for the boss swinging by our desks! New investing accounts were opened at record rates during the pandemic. Social media groups promoting investing strategies & early retirement exploded. My own kids started asking more questions about investing during that time. It's tough to not be influenced by the huge enthusiasm for it all. But, for most of us, early retirement is not reality!

The gamblers who lost money on the meme stocks during the pandemic aren't bragging & blogging about it anymore. Some newly inspired folk jumped on the FIRE bandwagon, but then had to go back & get a job. They don't get too much attention online these days. We tend to hear more from the successful ones that have huge followings on their blogs & social media channels. They can make money from their popularity. Some now have corporate sponsors & channel advertising revenue. Others are offering their services for money. They have turned their popularity into cash-generating businesses. Many of these people haven't taken early retirement, they're just doing something different now.

And kudos to them, it was a wonderful opportunity to capitalise on. But this will not be the reality for most of us.

Many who follow these successful FIRE folk are hoping that they can achieve the same lifestyle by putting everything they own into some high yield funds & not show up for work on Monday. It's not that easy. Come back to earth. Come back to your desk. Do the compounding & total return math very carefully before handing in your notice. If you can't do the math yourself, get help. You need to understand your true financial position & potential before taking such serious decisions. If you can't quit yet, don't despair. Just keep saving & investing for a retirement that might really work for you.

19. Alternative Strategies for Young & Old

Stock picking isn't for everyone. But, despite the long-term data supporting it, the market index investing approach may not suit everyone either. You can explore alternative strategies that suit your investor profile better. There will be as many combinations & permutations as there are investors, so I will use just one example here. This approach might suit someone scared by the markets & with a preference for lower volatility. Bond funds are not the only option to temper volatility. There are equity funds that favour such strategies too. Some of these ETFs can get long term results that are closer to market returns. While they may limit returns during times of exuberance, they can offer some downside protection during the bad times. One of the challenges for a DIY investor is to stay invested during the market cycles. At times, one strategy is abandoned at the lows, for another strategy that is hitting new highs. As we know, selling low & buying high is not a recipe for success. Different strategies will succeed at different times in the market cycles. And there may be differences within each market cycle. Chasing the current hot strategy will often result in poorer long-term results.

In this example, I'll use Vanguard's VGG & BMO's ZLU for US exposure. While not as broad as the market index, this combination of one dividend-growth fund & one low volatility fund diversifies the portfolio a little more than just going with either one of them. VGG was launched in the latter part of 2013, so let's look at the relative performance from 2014, up to early 2023. A $100k investment in the VFV market index ETF would be worth almost $316k today, an annualised return of 13.2%. While a 50:50 allocation to VGG & ZLU would have turned $100k into about $302k, for a CAGR of around 12.7%. That is not a bad relative performance for the alternate two-fund portfolio. Especially when you look at the volatility numbers. You can use measures like the standard deviation, beta, Sharpe & Sortino ratios, for relative volatility comparisons. We're not going into these measures here, but they are worth the effort of further study. The VGG-ZLU combo did better than VFV with all these volatility metrics. The combo's worst year over the 9-year period was a down year of just over 2%, while the worst year for the index was a down year of almost 14%. The maximum drawdown within a calendar year was over 13% for the combo portfolio, but the index was worse, at well over 18%. Across all those metrics, the combo portfolio showed lower volatility. While still providing a respectable return when compared to the index.

Now let's be real here. There are no guarantees that this performance, both in terms of returns & volatility, will be repeated going forward. But it's not unreasonable to consider the VGG-ZLU combo as a potentially better choice, for the US allocation, for an investor who worries about such things. These selections were just to illustrate the relative performance of two different investing styles. I didn't do an exhaustive search for this combo, so there may be better choices out there. If you have this, or any other strategy in mind, you'll have to do the legwork to find the best contenders in the space. But it does give you a feel for what you need to look for when you decide to depart from the market index strategy. With alternative choices, you should still look for low-fee options. Take your time, compare & choose carefully.

I'm not suggesting that you should never change strategies, by the way. As you learn more, & as life circumstances change, there may be good reason to make a change. But jumping from one strategy to another on the back of current trends is less likely to produce the result you are looking for. Plan & investigate your strategy changes well in advance of needing them. Back test trial portfolios to see if they worked the way you expected. Swapping in & out of strategies is another form of market timing. It's not something most of us do well.

20. Signing Off on Stocks

When it comes to investing, we all go through our own learning cycle. It's different for each of us & it can take a little or a long time to play out. Some are interested in learning more, others don't want to spend the time. In my case, I learned a little starting out & thought I knew a lot. I set out to beat the market with growth stocks & failed miserably. I played with some blue-chip dividend stocks but had no real appreciation for their potential & I abandoned them when I shouldn't have. I was not as courageous as I imagined I would be & I was scared out of the market by downturns & market crashes. Then I had no idea when to get back in. Nor what to invest in when I finally decided to go back in. Over the course of my investing life my education was hard won. It was expensive. And it's not over yet.

The more I learned, the more I realised that it's difficult to win by picking stocks. And stock picking takes a lot of extra work. Though my investing goals are changing as I edge closer to retirement, I have come to the conclusion that ETF investing is the way to go. For me. Being older, I tend to favour more conservative choices now. I can tolerate a lower-than-market return in exchange for a little less volatility. Though I had a good run with dividend growth investing, I now prefer to use ETFs. It's less worry & less work. On the other hand, there are many investors with exceptional dividend-growth stock portfolios that deliver a big & growing income stream. There are investors living the good life off the distributions from high yield funds. Each of us is different. There is no one-size-fits-all solution. We all need to figure out what works best for our circumstances & our mindset.

If you are fortunate enough to max out your TFSA & RRSP & are investing in a taxable account, there is one other thing to bear in mind. Generating taxable income prior to retirement, even with tax-advantaged Canadian dividends, isn't necessarily a good thing. ETFs with little or no distributions might be a better choice in a taxable account before you need that income. This may run contrary to your preferred strategy, but it can help reduce tax exposure during the working years prior to retirement. These can then be exchanged for income investments closer to, or after, retirement day.

Stock picking can be fun. But a portfolio built around a surprisingly small number of ETFs can serve many investors well too. It's less work & it will be less work for a surviving spouse & heirs. There are so many variables that it is impossible to provide a universal solution. But keeping it simple is usually not a bad thing.

Now you can breathe a sigh of relief, we're done with stocks. And there's much more fun stuff ahead!

Part 5 - Investing Outside the Markets

This really is a fun section. Though maybe more for me than for you. It includes all those little gems of parental advice that no kid ever listens to. But it's an opportunity for me to share some things that my kids will read years from now & when they do, they'll regret not having listened to me sooner. I'm kidding, I don't want that to be the case. So listen up, guys!

The real purpose of this section is see how a financial plan meshes with our overall plans for life. It includes some things that parents like to dish out advice on. As parents, we can suck at giving advice on many these areas too, of course.

But we're parents, we gotta give it a go, eh!

1. Job Hunting & Adventure

During my early years, it never struck me that being adventurous could have an impact on retirement. Living & working outside Canada can be a lot of fun. But it can have implications down the road.

The Canada Pension Plan (CPP) & Old Age Security (OAS) are the foundation of the income stream for most retirees in Canada. Both programs depend on living in Canada for 40 years for best results. To collect full CPP payments, you need to clock up 40 working years in Canada. And you must have enough years at the maximum contribution level to get the maximum pension. While you may be able to collect some pension income from other countries you've lived & worked in, it can make life easier if you can collect a full pension in Canada. Contributions in countries with a social security agreement with Canada may also fill those gaps.

To get the full OAS payment at 65, you only need to have lived in Canada for 40 years between ages 18 & 65. Work history doesn't matter for OAS. You can increase both government pensions by an incremental amount for every month you push off taking them, from age 65 up to a maximum of age 70. If you wait 'til 70, CPP is boosted by 42% & OAS by 36%. This adds a hefty additional amount to your basic pensions & since these are indexed, that could be very useful if you plan on living a long time after retiring. If you want to take advantage of that delay, you'll need enough savings & investments to fund those years between retirement & age 70. Or you could work all the way to age 70.

Now I'm not saying you shouldn't take an opportunity to live & work elsewhere. Travel is way too much fun to avoid for this reason. But it can work better if there is a reciprocal social security arrangement between Canada & that other country. Otherwise, there is the potential for reduced government pension income when you retire. Or you'll have to work out how to get additional pension payments from that other country. Of course, the other way you can reduce the importance of all this is to have a huge investment portfolio come retirement day. Save & invest early.

Your career choice can also have a huge impact on how you'll fare in retirement. We touched on this before, but a government job, or one of those rare private sector jobs with a defined benefit pension plan, looks a whole lot more appealing to me now. A defined benefit pension, with annual increases linked to inflation, wage growth, or the Consumer Price Index (CPI), is the holy grail for retirees. But many of us don't realise that until later in life. Working in the private sector, the best you can hope for these days is a defined contribution pension plan with an employer match. With a defined benefit plan, you know what you'll get out of it during retirement. Whereas you only know what you & your employer will put into a defined contribution plan. A DC plan does get you saving & investing, automatically, for retirement. That can be a very big deal. Especially if you're not getting around to doing any saving & investing yourself. When the employer matches the employees' contributions, you've got an immediate double. While you beaver away at the day job, your money can quietly double again in the background. That's doing the double double your money thing for real! Even if the returns within the plan aren't as good as the market, you're starting out way ahead. If you have any choice in the matter, choose the lowest cost, well-diversified index fund offered by your employer's pension plan. A job with a pension plan is very useful. But do your own saving & investing too.

Jobs with stock remuneration or stock options can also be a big deal. I knew more millionaires in the late 90s than I've ever known since. They worked for high-flying tech companies. The smart ones, or maybe they were just lucky, sold out before the dot-com crash. They are probably still millionaires. Some stuck with their hot stocks & much of their new paper wealth was erased when the bubble burst. If you work for a company & all your investments are in shares of the same company, that is a huge diversification risk. You could lose your job & your retirement portfolio all in one shot if the company goes belly up. Diversify!

Read on, there are a few other funny things to keep in mind if you keep putting off saving & investing for your retirement.

2. Get Married

Whether we like it or not, two can live cheaper than one. The increased savings possible with two incomes can make for a far more comfortable retirement than going it alone. Don't worry, I'm not going to start offering marital advice here. Or at least not much! But if you do find that perfect partner, there can be many advantages to doing things together.

When it comes to finding the right partner, try sharing the journey with a like-minded saver & investor. If you are a saver, that's a good thing. If your partner can't hang onto a paycheque past it hitting their bank account at the end of the month, your relationship might be challenged. For a marriage to work well, financially that is, I think that the spirit of frugality must be somewhat matched between both partners. If one wants to save aggressively, while the other is setting the credit card on fire, conflict will arise. If you are a saver & the love of your life is a spendthrift, get a prenup!

We all have our little quirks. For example, I dislike debt, intensely. Rather than invest, I favoured reducing the mortgage & having some emergency cash in the bank. Logic tells us that investing produces greater returns than the savings to be had from reducing low-cost mortgage debt. I didn't care. I didn't like debt. I was afraid of what would happen if I lost my job. Fortunately, my partner felt the same way & we were on the same page. Mostly! Had I married an investment advisor, things might have been different. Outside a few brief periods of insanity, I am far more comfortable living within my means. Though I didn't come to my senses on saving & investing 'til later in life, as a couple, my wife & I were generally in sync on the family finances.

Be aware that the cost of debt & the returns from the market aren't always aligned. Do you remember the earlier scenario we looked at? If you get a surprise lump sum, it may be more beneficial to pay down a 5% mortgage than to expect that the market will automatically give you a 10% return by investing it. All sorts of weird things can happen. The market might crash right after you invest. Maybe you'll lose your job right after that crash. Now you lose your house because you can't pay the mortgage. Under such awful circumstances, paying down the mortgage might have been the better choice. If debt, even lower cost debt, has the potential to expose you to a greater loss, think about reducing the debt before investing. Always be conscious of avoiding catastrophic loss.

Now, there are those who are quite happy to live life to the max. Even when that includes maxing out the credit cards & maxing out the line of credit. I will admit to occasional moments of envy. But I don't think this approach is well suited to building wealth. Though such folk certainly seem to enjoy driving new cars & taking off on extra winter breaks, I hope things hold up for them come retirement day. Look, I have no idea what the "right" approach to living life is. We all need to make that call for ourselves. But one thing I am pretty sure of is that both partners need to be in the same ballpark on the major principles of finance. If partners are pulling in opposite directions on something as serious as the financial stability of the family, something will break.

Assuming you have all that in sync, the next steps are important. In anticipation of a divorce, you should each have your own TFSA & RRSP accounts. I'm kidding about the divorce thing, I hope you'll choose each other well & have a long & happy life together. But from a purely financial perspective, you **both** need **all** those accounts anyway. In order to maximise the tax sheltering advantages that are available to each partner & to the family. There may be estate planning & other advantages to a joint non-registered investment account. Ask your lawyer about estate planning when you're having your will drawn up. Though there are rules about who contributed how much, you can split income from investments in a joint taxable account. That might be of value if one partner earns more than the other. Or when one parent takes time off work to raise children.

I believe in love at first sight, but my wife doesn't. Sometimes, I wonder how we made it this far. But we did. Fingers crossed, touch wood, it will continue that way. The numbers don't look half as good if we need to split & start over as singles! Starting out, going through life, & all the way to the end, two can more profitably live together than one. Sticking together through thick & thin does pay dividends.

Couldn't help that one, sorry! LOL

Get married, enjoy life, be nice to each other, & don't make mountains out of mole hills. Except for your portfolio. Save & invest so you can do all the things you want to do, but with a little less worry.

For all other marital advice, go to your favourite social media site.

You know I'm kidding with that one, right!?!

3. Relationships

We're done with the marriage talk; this is about friends & family. It's a lot easier to move about the world these days. I've lived in a few countries over the course of my life & I've moved around inside all of those. While I have thoroughly enjoyed all the travel & making new friends in new places, I have left many friends behind. Sadly, I have lost some good friends along the way too. Life really is too short sometimes. Though social media allows me to connect with friends over long distances, there is nothing like being able to spend Saturday morning having coffee with an old friend.

I wish some of my departed friends were still around. I wish I lived closer to some others who still are. If you see me sitting alone in a café one Saturday morning, please come join me. I'm always open to making new friends too.

Invest in your relationships with family & friends. I know this sounds like excruciatingly boring, old-person, greeting-card philosophy nonsense. But I can guarantee that you will find your relationships are one of your most precious assets as you get older.

There's always that one irritating or irresponsible family member, of course. But we need them too. They are perfect subjects for the family gossip sessions!

4. Striking a Balance

I think I made a bit of a mess of the whole work-life balance thing. Somehow, work things always seem to have found their way onto my calendar before matters that were of greater importance. I shy away from analysing this more, because I think the self-recrimination might be a bit harsh. I've been attending our big annual industry trade show for more than 25 years now. As soon as one year's show is done & dusted, I've got next year's on the calendar. The timing sometimes meant that a family spring break was postponed. Or cancelled. I did this because this show was so important. And my absence would be noticed. The covid lockdown eliminated the show for a couple of years & when it resumed, I didn't attend the first one. For the first time in decades. What surprised me most about not attending was how few people noticed that I wasn't there. What an ego crusher that was. Nobody gave a duck. Serves me right, eh!

Some of us are driven by what we do & we sometimes forget who we are. Or who we want to be. I have no further suggestions on how you should do this better. But it does merit some thought. Of course, I am not suggesting that you should open a job interview by telling your prospective employer that you work to live & not live to work! If you need the job, let them tell you that they encourage a work-life balance. This is more likely to occur with good employers. Or during those rare times when people are more scarce than jobs. Some companies just don't work that way & it's all about the job. But some people like it that way too. Your call.

The whole balance thing occurs in many parts of our lives. Including the work that surrounds saving & investing. When we partner up, for example, we tend to divide the workload based on preferences & on skillsets. And on who is better at avoiding doing those things they don't like to do. If A brings the garbage out, B brings the dog out. A does the cooking, B does the cleaning. Go ahead, short-change yourself by not learning how to cook if you like! But when it comes to managing money, you **both** need to be good at it. This kind of balance should be a law of personal finance.

If you leave all the money management in the hands of one partner, the other partner is exposed to significant risk. Especially if the financial manager in the household dies first. And without leaving a clear set of instructions behind. Advisors love it when an ignorant survivor walks into their office with a big portfolio!

When it comes to your financial plan, you **both** need to know what you are doing. Why you are doing it. And you each need to have the required skills to carry on with the plan, should you lose your partner or separate. Forget about date nights to keep the romance alive. Instead, schedule regular financial dates to ensure that you're both in the loop on how to manage your finances. Make sure you ticked the right box, so that the TFSA & RRSP accounts are set up to roll into the surviving spouse's accounts without getting mauled by the taxman. Talk to your brokerage or advisor to make sure you checked all the right boxes. It's that important. You want the surviving spouse to get all tax-sheltered funds, from the dead guy's accounts, rolled into the survivor's tax-sheltered accounts. And all **without** any tax exposure or loss of future sheltering.

Okay, I was just kidding about forgetting date night.

Both partners should have all the typical investing accounts, but I'm not suggesting that you live separate financial lives. You can figure out how to share income & expenses on your own. But with tax-sheltered investment accounts, pay attention to balancing a future income stream. If one partner leaves the workforce to raise kids, for example, then the remaining income earner might want to contribute to a spousal RRSP. The high-income earner gets the tax relief &, as a couple, you get closer to retirement with two similar RRSP amounts. This is useful for balancing the tax burden if you need to withdraw from the RRSP accounts before reaching age 65. Note that spousal contributions can't be withdrawn for three years (look up the spousal RRSP attribution rules on the CRA site), or the tax burden falls back on the contributor. After 65, income splitting though a RRIF (Registered Retirement Income Fund) is easier, but who knows what things will look like by the time you retire. There's a lot more to this. Taxation in retirement can be quite messy, so see your tax advisor & financial planner if you don't learn enough to plan an efficient withdrawal strategy yourself. And have that meeting well ahead of retirement, in case you need to restructure things a bit before abandoning working life. Paying less tax is good for both partners.

Divorce statistics are high. I hope you enjoy each others company enough that you won't ever need to become part of that statistical cohort. But should you ever decide to divorce, it should be a little easier to get through if you both have your finances in balance. And if you both know how to manage your money going forward. Invest time in learning how to do that from the get-go & you might remain friends after the divorce. That can be important too.

I can't finish off talking about divorce, can I? Instead, let me wish you every success in love, life & work. And with your investments. I hope you can strike the right balance & may you have many happy anniversaries to look forward to.

5. Should You Buy a House?

Because of the wealth generated by home ownership in Canada over the years, the answer is somewhere between definitely & maybe. This may be obvious, but you should only buy a home if you can afford it. And if you have confidence that you can keep up with the mortgage payments during times of financial stress. It helps if you have an emergency fund in place to cover things like job loss. You might not want to own a home if you are just starting out on your career path & you expect to move around a lot to get established. Or if you just haven't made up your mind about where you'd like to live yet. Owning a home for a short time could see the transaction costs being more than the price appreciation on the house. Fees matter with houses too. Buying at the wrong time might mean you'll have to sell at a loss to move to that new job. Is now a good time to buy a house? I have no idea. I don't have a crystal ball for predicting the future of the housing market either. On the other hand, if you decide to rent, you should start saving & investing right away. You'll have no other asset that is appreciating in value. But that's probably in your financial plan already, right?

And there's the crux of the problem for most of us. We don't start out with a financial plan. Creating a lifelong financial plan will help get your head around what's important for you. And it will help you put things in priority order. A kid with rich parents & a secure job at the family business may well choose to go for the house first. But others might focus on getting an emergency fund in place first. Then a foundational investment portfolio. And next comes the house. The thing about building a financial plan *first* is that it gets you thinking about the risks & rewards of all the different options that are available for *you*.

Once you get around to buying a home, the history of property value appreciation in Canada makes a house not just a home, but a decent investment to boot. Real estate, including the primary home, is a great wealth diversifier. Most of us need a mortgage to support the purchase. That is leveraged investing. Leverage is when you borrow money to invest. That's a risky proposition. Either for stocks or for a home. When it comes to buying a home, we do it because we want a place to live. A place to call home. And because almost everyone else does it! But most of us are buying a home, not an investment property.

While some are comfortable with leveraged investing, I wouldn't borrow money to invest in the market. But I never had any problem taking on a mortgage to buy a home. It's an emotional thing, what can I say. Might as well pay a mortgage, rather than rent, eh? A beneficial side effect is that borrowing to buy a house is an enforced savings & leveraged investing program for many. There's that automation thing again. If you can't get around to saving & investing for retirement … you might want to buy a house!

Houses are like stocks in that they tend to provide better return when held for the long haul. But did you know that the stock market, even the humble Canadian index, outperforms home ownership returns? Though some housing markets in Canada have done phenomenally well in recent years. While we don't get any tax relief on mortgage interest payments in Canada, the capital gains on the primary residence are tax free. That's a big deal. Outside of the TFSA or a lottery win, I think it's the only other investment that can generate tax-free returns. This only applies to the primary residence. Not to additional holiday or rental properties. You do need to report the purchase & sale of your primary residence to the CRA. Though you are not taxed on any capital gains, you can be penalised if you don't report the transactions & fill out the right forms.

Starting out, put a financial plan together *first*. Make home buying *part* of that financial plan. Once you pull the trigger, mortgage payments will eat into your disposable & investable income. That makes it even more important to get something invested in the market at the earliest possible opportunity. Right behind an emergency fund, building a little investment portfolio might be next on the list. Then buy a house.

There are some other considerations though.

6. Home Ownership Considerations

If you have a partner sharing the cost of home ownership, so much the better. If you both work at different companies, that mitigates the risks of both income generators losing a job at the same time. Nobody wants to lose their home following the loss of a job. Looking back, I never had a problem owning a home. My problem is that I've owned too many of them! Moving frequently meant that I paid a lot of fees for all those real estate transactions. The lost opportunity cost of all those fees is huge. I can't bear thinking about it. Though if I'd stayed put, I'd probably have squandered all the saved cash on other silly things anyway. That's what happens when you don't have a financial plan. There were some legitimate moves, like changing countries & provinces for adventure or for a new job. Hey, adventure is important for some people! But most moves were just ego driven. I wanted a bigger, flashier house. I was out to impress. You know what? The world didn't give a flying duck! I can't say that I didn't enjoy all my houses along the way. But I can think of at least 4 moves that were just a pure & unnecessary money drain. If I had the opportunity to do it all over again, I would do it differently. And I would certainly move a whole lot less. Circumstances are different for everyone. But, with hindsight, moving less & investing more would have been a far better approach. Had I done that, the Joneses might be jealous now!

Along with buying & selling too frequently, I generally bought the most house I could afford in the early years. I now think this was a really bad idea. Sure, I could brag about my nice new house. But it also restricted cash flow until my career & income got me ahead of the curve again. At which time I bought a bigger house & maxed everything out again. Of course, I needed a new car to match the new house. Another silly mistake. I really wasn't impressing anyone. Because no-one really cared. Ego can be costly.

Being house poor is not always the best way to grow wealth. When I finally got sense, I started downsizing. Sometimes in anticipation of a big housing market crash. A few downsizing moves later, the housing crash still hasn't happened. Turns out that predicting the direction of the housing market is about as challenging as timing the stock market. If I had a do-over, I would stick with my smaller starter house for longer. I would invest all those real estate & moving fees instead.

I would not like starting out in today's expensive housing market. But it felt like that back then too. If I had that do-over, no matter how big a mortgage the bank approved, I'd buy a house that needed less than that. And I would invest a little instead. Forget about impressing the neighbours. Impress yourself by building wealth that nobody can see but you. Be the iceberg!

The biggest disadvantage of owning a home is that you must do all that DIY stuff. I think I know how to do all that &, on paper, I do. My Dad was brilliant with his hands. But I'm useless. I'm also quite lazy. I am a half-decent painter but anything else takes six months of study & planning. Then I screw things up so many times that I spend huge amounts of time running back & forth to the hardware store for fresh supplies & missing tools. I have an amazing collection of tools for sale if you're interested. Many are in like-new condition! Maybe that's why we changed houses so often? Seems like we sold most of our houses just ahead of when they might need work.

During all my early years of home ownership, I never had much of a financial plan. I never had a clear vision for saving & investing for retirement. If I could go back, I would prepare my financial plan *first*! Even if my plan was as simple as just saving & investing enough to give me a shot at hitting a target number far away in the future. Once that was in play, I would then integrate the purchase of a home into that financial plan. My savings rate would have dropped when mortgage payments started. Maybe no savings at all for a few years. But had I been thinking that way, had I been more focused on a financial plan that was based on a foundational investment portfolio & a long-term view, I might have considered cheaper properties. I might have chosen a home that would have enabled me to save & invest a little all the way through. Even if it were just a tiny amount to maintain the habit. In those very early years, I might even have chosen a home with a rentable room or basement, so that someone else could help pay down my mortgage. Putting the financial plan together should come first. Everything that follows will be viewed a little differently then.

My wife & I briefly considered an income property. A lot of people have made a lot of money following this path. We decided not to go through with it & we walked away from a small apartment building. It had three apartments. We would have lived in one unit, while renting the other two. Looking back on it now, this could have been one of the best financial moves we ever almost made. But, given how poor my DIY skills subsequently proved to be, it might have been a disaster. Renting out property comes with a whole host of other challenges. Including the potential for renting out to the tenants from hell, tax reporting, & who knows what else. If you are up for tackling those challenges, then an income property might be a great way to go. If that's not for you, you could just buy some REIT ETF shares for that real estate exposure instead.

There are many other costs involved with owning a home. Insurance, taxes, repairs, & so on. We tend to let those fade into the background when we look at how well our home appreciated in value over time. For long time homeowners, the difference between cost & current value can be very dramatic. It can also be a bit of an illusion. Plug these number into an online CAGR calculator to see what the annualised appreciation really was. From the "home as an investment" perspective, CAGR is the best way to understand the value of home appreciation too. You should then deduct a percent or two from the CAGR number to cover all those other support & maintenance costs.

Despite all the money I threw away on moving so often, home ownership has been a net positive over the years. Emotionally & financially. Even with the insane home prices these days, I think home ownership can be a good thing for many people. If only because so many people won't save & invest early enough. Just be careful not to bite off more than you can chew when it comes to the size of the mortgage payment. Always be ready for the next huge bump in mortgage interest rates. You don't want to be panic selling when many others are doing the same. It's just like the stock market, eh!

Are house prices going to crash now? I have no idea. But if they do, buying a home after a big crash could be useful. Houses, like stocks, provide better returns when you get them cheap.

7. Bad Habits

Imagine a twenty-year old saving & investing on a regular basis. The process is automated & runs like a clock. Everything is on track. But he, or she, smokes cigarettes! I won't bore you with the health admonitions, but a pack-a-day habit, at $20 a pack, will cost our young investor more than six million dollars by retirement day.

OMG, I feel so stupid sometimes!

Okay, I know you don't need the drugs & booze speech, but there are other socially acceptable habits that can fly under the frugal investor's radar. It's awfully easy to get into routines of eating lunch out every day. Or a habit of drinking expensive frappalattamochachais. Use your compound growth app to evaluate any habit that costs you money on a regular basis. If giving up your visits to the café is impossible, try drinking something cheaper. Like regular coffee. Or water. If that's too embarrassing, just pretend you're some kind of health nut. Maybe you're fasting or doing keto. Come up with something, anything, to avoid squandering money that could be invested instead. At least until you have that foundational amount invested. You should aggressively chase getting that foundational amount invested.

Watch out for those monthly paid services too. The reason every company wants us to switch to a subscription model these days is because it's so profitable. For them. Especially the nested streaming or gaming type services, where we can add other channels & services inside the primary service. Do we really need half a dozen paid streaming apps? Cancel these services & buy shares of the companies selling them instead.

There are many things we squander money on. Squandering is, by definition, wasteful. Though I admit, it can be fun. But it can also take away from our ability to reach a level of wealth where we can more easily enjoy a broader selection of the nicer things that life can offer. Don't misunderstand this, I am not suggesting that you give up all those things you love. Instead, be selective. Spend your available time & money on those things that bring you the greatest joy. Delay the gratification for some of those choices that matter less. Once you meet your financial obligations **and** your saving & investing goals on a weekly or monthly basis, you can enjoy squandering the rest.

We all like our toys. No point in trying to talk you out of whatever your toy addiction is. Go ahead, enjoy your toys. I used to think that all that stuff about experiences being more precious than things was just more new-age blather.

It's just downright embarrassing how often I'm wrong!

8. Investing in Yourself

My parents struggled to pay for my education. But they made the sacrifices & they did it. I'm grateful to them. We used Registered Education Savings Plans (RESPs) to help pay for our kids' education. With hindsight, the investment choices inside the RESPs weren't the best. But it worked out okay anyway. Because the competition can be so fierce these days, a primary degree opens fewer doors than it used to. But it still helps. Maybe you'll need two! If you want higher education, try doing it right after high school. It can be a total grind to have to go back for further education later in life. Although if that's what you feel you need to do, do it. An education is rarely a waste. The process of education teaches you more than the subject matter. It teaches you how to learn. That skill is with you for life. If you have an engineering degree, but you prefer to work in café for your day job, that's totally your call. If further education is not for you, that's okay too. Read more. Do more. Live more. Learning doesn't only happen at a university. Some people love working with their hands. And tradespeople often find it easier to start a sustainable business than those with a degree. Some who study music become rock stars. Some who learn to play the guitar in their basements become rock stars too! With education, as with investing, there is no one-size-fits-all program. In general though, the higher the level of education, the bigger the retirement portfolio. If you choose to leave school earlier, buck that trend by saving & investing earlier. You now know how to beat those odds!

There's a lot of fluff out there about investing in yourself. If I was absolutely, amazingly, astoundingly, brilliant at something, I would have been discovered already. Sure, I like to tell myself I do some things well. Perhaps even better than many others. But, cruel as it is to admit, I'm probably pretty average. On the other hand, I think I'm average at way more things than the average person! It's a struggle to remember exactly how I thought at your age, but being a dilettante is probably not what I dreamed of becoming back then. It takes an incredible amount of focus to dedicate yourself to one thing & to become great at it. Most of us won't do it. Some people have natural gifts. There are those who vault to the forefront courtesy of the life they were born into. While still others' achievements are the consequence of parental obsession. I've already apologised to my kids for not being rich & famous enough to save them the trouble of having to do it all for themselves. And that I wasn't obsessed enough to force them to excel at something. It's down to them, & to you, to uncover any hidden natural gifts. And to become obsessed about something. But if all that sounds like too much work, what else can you do?

Outside of saving & investing regularly?

Damned if I know!

9. Luck & Passion

There's a whole industry & social following surrounding the notion that if you do what you're passionate about, you'll never work a day in your life. And that you'll magically make a ton of money being passionate. What a load of ducky doo-doo. Don't worry if you are feeling left out of the passion game Not all, but a lot of people are faking it!

I have been very passionate about so many things over the course of my life. But they all faded. Was I just not committed enough? Or have I not found that perfect, enduring, all-consuming passion yet? Were those things not really a passion? I don't know, but I'm not going to waste any more time looking. Life is too short.

I took up golf when I was 40. I was accidentally signed up for a best-ball tournament at a sales event. I didn't even know what a "best-ball" tournament was. My colleagues talked me into sticking with it. At the first tee, that small ball against me? I couldn't resist crushing the little thing into the next county. With the first mighty swing, I wound up on my arse, on the ground. While the little ball still sat on the tee. Laughing at me. I eventually got the ball off the tee but, by the end of the 18 holes, I think I'd only made about two good strokes all day. But those two stokes were so sublime that I was seduced. I came back home, bought all the gear, & headed to the driving range. Every day. For about 3 months. My hands bled from hitting balls. I then took my new gear & my bloody hands to a small local golf course. I got around in something over 150 strokes. For non-golfers, par is 72, so that's a little high! But, in my defence, I am a scrupulously honest golfer. I then went out alone & walked 9 holes, every morning, before work, for the remainder of the season. I was hooked. Addicted. Passionate. Next season I got below 100 for the first time & I was off buying new clubs already. I went for lessons. I read books. I watched videos. You name it, if I thought it could improve my golf game, I was buying it, doing it, living & breathing it. By the third or fourth season my handicap was somewhere in the high teens & I think I had my first (was that my only?) round in the seventies. Surely, I was bound for the professional tour. That didn't happen. The golf gods mocked me & my handicap drifted back up. Some years later, my passion evaporated. Success, however fleeting, fed the passion. Though I've decluttered heavily in recent years, I kept all my golf gear. Who knows when the passion might rekindle. Maybe I'll make it on some local senior tour during retirement!

In my day job, while I've changed jobs & roles, I've stuck with the same industry for my entire career. I've had brief periods of exhilaration. And a few bouts with anxiety & despair. But it's mostly been an enjoyable grind that floats around the midpoint where it's generally not bad. Our little company did well at the end of the nineties, the tech boom. Had that tech bubble not burst & had foreign outsourcing not become a thing, I might have made millions. That didn't happen either. But if it had, I'm sure I would be a lot more passionate about it all today. We tempted fate with a few new products that could have been huge. Had even one of those come off, I think I would have maintained far greater passion. We can debate whether I & my colleagues had the skills necessary to make it all happen, or not. But I like to think that the only thing missing was a bit of good luck. We continue to work hard & cross our fingers. Waiting for the luck & the passion to strike.

Whatever you do, try to do it well.

Do anything well enough, for long enough, & you'll continue to improve. That's true of just about everything in life. Except maybe golf. You don't need to have passion for what you do, but you do need a good attitude. No matter what you do, dedicate yourself to doing it a little better. Every day. People will notice how good you are. And that will make you feel better. The better you get, the better you feel. And the more passion you will experience. Regardless of what you do, if you are the best in your field, you may be appropriately rewarded & you will reverse engineer some feeling of passion for what you do. Now, depending on what you get good at, that doesn't automatically come with riches. You'll notice I said "appropriately" rewarded, not fairly rewarded. Life isn't always fair, get over it. You may brew a really good cup of coffee, but the guy who perfects steering a hockey puck into the opponent's net will probably get paid more than you.

If you happen to not be totally in love with your day job, make sure you lie about that! I'm not kidding, do not *ever* tell *anyone* that your job sucks. Don't even say that to yourself. It's very unlucky. You know not to tell your boss, but don't say that to your best friend on the job either. Even if they talk about how much they hate their jobs, do not join them in denigrating what you do. You should never say out loud that you dislike your job. Aside from reinforcing the negativity in your own mind, the opportunity for things to come back to bite you down the road is huge. Why am I drivelling on about all this stuff? Because you create your own universe inside your head. Try keeping your head in a place you enjoy hanging out in. Smile & encourage yourself to enjoy what you do. It doesn't work all the time, but you'll probably get lucky with it every now & then.

None of this applies if you are being harassed or mistreated in any way, of course. Seek help & get out of that kind of situation immediately. Outside of that terrible circumstance, if you truly feel unhappy in your job, & if you feel there is no escape right now, you should still try to improve doing whatever you do. But you need to get good at something else too. For the sake of your sanity & your self-esteem. I don't know, maybe pick a hobby you like & one you know you can do well with. Spend time with friends off the job. Find something, anything, that will keep you going while you search for another job or career path.

Perhaps you could practice being a great saver & investor? While it may take 10 or 20 years to prove it, you might get pretty lucky with that.

10. Starting a Business

Most of us shouldn't start a business. I wish I was kidding, but statistics suggest it's true. About one quarter of start-ups don't get past the first year. More than half of new businesses are gone within three years. Less than one in five survives to the ten-year mark. This is all just too bloody awful, isn't it?

Starting a business is exciting but it's tough. New, small, start-ups are particularly vulnerable. If the business is easy to get into, it'll be easier for it to fail. Starting a business with a smaller budget than the competition exposes it to more risk. Starting a business without knowing what the market wants won't work. People with trade skills seem to be pretty successful with solo operations. Electricians, carpenters, plumbers, hairdressers, landscapers, & so on are common in the small business community. Some are happy doing their own thing, while others will add more people & build a company. Starting a business with one or more partners has some advantages. There are more people contributing to the cost of getting things up & running. You have colleagues right out of the gate so there is built-in coverage for illness & some vacation time. And a greater range of skillsets is brought to bear. Just behind our primary personal relationships, business partnerships are probably the most critical & challenging relationships in our lives. The divorce rate is high in business circles too. Be careful who you get into bed with.

Am I telling you to never start your own business? Absolutely not, I've loved every business venture I've ever been involved with & I think it's a great thing to consider. But first you should put some time into understanding the risks. Between us, my wife & I have owned some or all of half a dozen or so small business ventures over the years. Some were small gig ventures & the cost of entry was low. They didn't need to make money, so they don't really count. My wife did better than I did with these. Three were raw start-ups that needed to pay wages & rent. Two failed during the start-up phase & the third succeeded. Though we had moved on from the successful one, I think it may have closed the doors during covid. Who could have seen that covid lockdown thing coming, eh? The remaining two were purchases of existing businesses. We remain involved in only one, but both are still doing their thing today. Though this is too small a sample size to be statistically useful, it's interesting to see the higher failure rate of the raw start-ups. Compared to that of existing businesses with a track record. In addition to our own endeavours, I've been involved in working with other people's start-ups too. Some made it, some didn't. Failure is a common theme in the start-up world but the ones that made it are having a lot of fun. The bottom line is that you need to carefully weight up your options before embarking on a business venture.

I've heard so many people talk about opening restaurants & cafés over the years, you'd think it was as hot a space as green energy or AI. It looks easy, so just about anyone that can brew coffee thinks they can do it. Once or twice, I even contemplated that myself. But my passion for sitting around drinking coffee & chatting with people all day wasn't a qualification for starting a coffee shop. The café idea is also not expensive compared to many other businesses. That is a weakness. I'm not picking on this business for any reason, it's just by way of example. It's one that appeals to many of us & it is relatively affordable. If starting a business is affordable, many potential competitors can afford to get into it too. You shouldn't be surprised to hear that this sector has one of the highest failure rates. We can all fry an egg & make coffee. That does not mean we're going to found the next great fast-food chain. On the other hand, it doesn't mean you can't.

I saw a post on social media yesterday (total coincidence but very timely), where a young man was outlining his education & skills. His post went on to ask for suggestions on what business he should start that would make money. For his sake I hope I'm wrong, but I think that's putting a little too much faith in the hive-mind. If you feel compelled to start a business, without a clear vision of what makes for a desirable product, for a sufficiently large audience, do something that costs next to nothing & gig it. Because it will be more likely to fail. Maybe you could try being a social media influencer. That costs next to nothing & who knows, you might get lucky!

This is observational & again, it's from too small a sample size to be statistically useful. But from my own ventures & from those of some others I've worked with, it seems like everything is a double-double. And not in the compound growth sense. It's the time & money part of most business plans. Using all the rules of good business planning, you create the perfect business plan. When the plan goes from paper to the real world, it always takes twice as long & costs twice as much to implement. Even when the plan is supposed to include allowances for such things. If you ever put a business plan together, I'll be happy to review it for you. I'll just take my large red felt pen & put a big "2X" on the cost & time pages. If you've got the extra time & money to cover that, maybe you should go for it. Unfortunately, I've seen some failures that might have been successful. If they'd only had the money to stick with it for a bit longer.

Write your business plan. Then compare the potential return on an investment in your business to that of buying an index fund. The index fund is filled with existing businesses that have made it past the start-up danger zone.

Invest your time & money wisely!

11. The Next Big Thing

If any industry can figure out how to package something for profit, it's the financial services industry. Until any of these products are old & mature enough, with a history of good performance, it might be wise to steer clear. Private equity, IPOs, SPACs, crypto, & famous people stuff are all on my avoid list. I'm not saying that people haven't made money in any of these areas. But, because of my limited knowledge & insight, I'd rather go to the casino. There, at least, I might get free drinks while I lose my money. It's easy to be lured by the marketing messages for the next big thing. Take your time & let the sales pitch mature in your mind. Before you act on anything new that promises incredible success. Many don't deliver. Some of the purveyors aren't much more than sharp salespeople. Some of them might even turn out to be swindlers. While I didn't invest in anything like this, I am guilty of wasting a few bucks on get-rich-quick courses over the years. Despite how often I say "never say never", I'll make an exception for this kind of stuff & say: never again!

Now I came very close to succumbing to a sales pitch from a private real estate equity investment company way back. Sharp-dressed, professional salesperson. Got introduced to the very personable & professional guy heading up the company. And to some of the existing investors. Who were far savvier & more qualified in the investing space than I was. All in all, it was a pretty convincing sales pitch, developed over the course of a year or more. I wish I could say that I was so smart that I knew it wasn't a good investment right off the bat. In reality, I was really tempted. And they were spinning a great story. The only reason I didn't go in was the lack of detailed financial information on the website. And there were no other documents available to make up for that lack of info. Only more sales talk. Not that I could have interpreted that final information very well, but its absence made me nervous. Because I was still dithering on making my decision, I delayed long enough for the whole thing to collapse. Talk about luck! There are too many good investment opportunities available in the public markets to take the risk of going with some guy knocking on your door with a good sales pitch.

Stick to your knitting. Invest in yourself. Invest in a home. And invest in the market by building a portfolio that will let you sleep reasonably well at night. That approach has been more consistently successful for more people over time.

Looks like the next big thing is going to be AI. It'll be interesting to watch the marketing blurb roll out on that one. It sounds just like the internet bubble in the late 90s. Already I'm ignoring it. AI will be everywhere. But it'll be used by most of the companies in my index ETFs too. I'll just take whatever returns that come from that.

12. The Big Picture

We have covered a few things in this section that are important components of all our lives. While I've been burned by some experiences, I've been lucky with others. Outside of those experiences, I have no special insights on any of these very challenging & complex areas of life. I conveniently avoided some other really important areas, like spirituality, physical & mental wellbeing, & so on. Though I have prayed for my portfolio on occasion, the purpose here was not to get into some of these hugely significant areas of living a fuller life. Instead, it is to think about the importance of including a financial plan as part of your overall life strategy. For whatever reason, we seem to stick saving & investing into its own little box. Then we push it off to the side as we get on with our "real" lives. While we are encouraged to think about many of those other very important aspects of our lives from an early age, it might be useful to integrate financial planning from a young age too. It is an important part of the life puzzle we are all trying to put together. Make sure a financial plan is part of your process & part of your life. Right from the start.

Enough of the heavy stuff, let's continue with some silly things now. Including some pointers that might help you get started. No point in reading all this if you're not going to do anything afterwards, eh!?!

Part 6 – Tying Up the Loose Ends

Most books build up to a crescendo. A thrilling climax to close out the story. I was hoping my portfolio would be worth gazillions by the time I finished this book. That would have been an impressive way to finish. A multi-million-dollar flourish to prove it all works. But, darn it, that didn't happen.

I should have started saving & investing earlier!

So instead of a climax, this final section is a collection of bits & pieces that didn't quite fit in the other sections. It also includes some final words of encouragement. Especially to my own kids, who probably skipped over half the chapters in here. And since I'm a Dad, I'm probably going to repeat some stuff. It's what Dads do, sorry!

I'll also tell you why there's a duck on the cover!

1. Tell Me What to Do!

I can't tell you what to invest in, only you can decide what works for you. It's tough to figure out what kind of investor you are 'til you've been investing for a while. You can read all about it, but you won't know how you will react to markets, bull & bear, until you live through a few market cycles. And you may react differently as you get older, as the size of your portfolio changes, & as your life circumstances change.

All you can do starting out is to pick a strategy that aligns with your best estimate of what kind of investor you are. Complete some of the "investor questionnaires" online. Vanguard Canada, BMO, & other sites offer these. Without the need to give your name & email address. Complete 3 or 4 of these & review the results. That will give you some idea of your investor profile & a recommended portfolio allocation model. Start by investing in one or more of the well-diversified ETFs that match your profile. Don't use money that you will need for any other purposes over the next several years.

A more aggressive profile result might suggest an all-equity portfolio. Historically, taking on more risk has delivered more reward. That could align with the North American index strategy, but it's more likely you'll be recommended a portfolio with greater diversification. You might be able to go with one of the globally diversified all-equity funds. Depending on your age & risk tolerance, you could get a recommendation for a bond allocation. Then you can buy one of the all-in-one funds with a bond allocation. You should retake these questionnaires periodically. Over time you'll probably adjust your answers based on your experiences in the market. That's fine, it's what happens for most of us.

If you can't get past all those feelings of uncertainty & you still can't get invested, you should see an advisor. Yes, it will cost you more. But if you need the help & encouragement, there is nothing wrong with paying for that to get you started. Try not to pay too much though. If the advisor's strategy works, you can always copy that in a DIY account later. Aside from paying attention to costs & fees, the **only** thing you control in this whole process is your savings rate. Only you control how much you save from every paycheque. Pick a number of dollars, or a number of hours worth of work, to save from every paycheque & ***automate*** your savings process. Do this at least. Automating this habit is one of the most important things you can do.

If investing is new for you, all of this can be a lot to digest, I know. It can be tough to get started. Look, there are no guarantees here, but I don't know a better alternative. I like the idea of owning shares in some of the world's biggest & best companies. It's reassuring to know that some very smart people are out there working for me. Every hour of every day. I hope they will continue to do that for you too.

2. Know What You're Doing

While I can't tell you what to do, make sure you know what you plan to do starting out. The simpler it is, the easier it is to accomplish that. If you have just one ETF in mind, like XEQT, VGRO, or ZBAL, for example, it's easy. You are just going to buy that same ETF every time. If you are going to buy more than one, then know exactly what percentage of each you want in your portfolio. Have a destination account in mind for every savings transfer. If you are focused on getting the TFSA spun up first, then you have only one account to worry about. If you want to utilise the TFSA & RRSP during the course of one year, plan what goes where in advance, so you're not procrastinating along the way. Do all this planning before you start. But don't let the investment planning exercise be a procrastination excuse to delay getting your automated savings program in place. If you decide to go with an advisor, more of the planning burden usually falls to them. You just need to get your money over there on a regular basis.

I won't go on about it anymore, you know what I'm talking about here. Automation & habituation are easier to establish when you know what you're doing ahead of time.

3. How Much Should You Save?

You can get rich by saving one hour's worth of wages a week. That sounds great, but it's perhaps a little too optimistic. The best thing about only saving one hour's wages a week is that it's better than saving nothing at all. The real question is more about if your savings rate is enough to achieve your goals. While some people are enjoying blowing everything they earn, there are extreme savers who save the equivalent of twenty or thirty hours of their weekly income. Some are so dedicated that they will take on a second job & save the income from that job too. They are happy to endure a modest & frugal lifestyle to meet their aggressive savings objectives. This is more common among those seeking very early retirement.

Somewhere between these two extremes will be more comfortable for most of us. I'd hate to live a miserably frugal young life & then die before retirement. Even with a huge portfolio. Life should be lived today, every day, all the way through.

Earlier, we looked at a simple example of creating a target retirement amount based on current income & using the 4% rule. It's as good a way as any to set an initial target. In your twenties, you should have an interim savings target to hit by age thirty. When you reach thirty, re-evaluate everything & set a new savings target to reach by age forty. These should be savings targets, not portfolio value targets. The market will do what it can with your investment choices in every decade. Some decades might be great, some not so great. But in each of these decades, you will likely change the number of hours of income you want to save. You can save a higher percentage of income before you take on a mortgage, less afterwards, so be flexible. Don't yell at yourself when your savings rate must go down. And you might not ever need to if you get a foundational amount invested early enough. And then leave it alone to do its thing.

When you first start working, the urge to spend is huge. It is so easy to blow it all. The automated savings process should protect you from that. Saving something consistently, no matter how small, is a great habit to put in place right away. But the question becomes: how many hours worth of work should you save?

Your life, your target, your choice. If you can't figure it out quickly, just pick a number & go. It's far too easy to waste a decade or two trying to figure out what that number should be. If you are totally paralysed by the decision & you want me to pick a number for you, go with six hours worth to start. That's 15% of your income, based on a forty-hour week.

That doesn't work for you?

Okay, pick your own darn number then!

4. Investing or Betting?

If you know what you are buying & why you are buying it, you are investing. If you would be okay letting your portfolio do its thing while you were stranded on a desert island for 20 years, that's an investing plan that will let you sleep at night. With investing, you have a strategy, a plan, & a process to follow. If you are buying low-cost, index ETFs, with a view to not touching them for years, you are on about as solid a foundation as you will find in this game. You are investing.

Beyond that, you might need to learn some stuff before you can pick stocks. If you are picking stocks based on a buddy's recommendation, a TV show, or a social media guru, you're gambling. If you "feel" something is a good investment, you're not just gambling, you're dreaming. I'm not saying feelings don't have a part to play. Just not like this. During moments of market euphoria, high-flying stocks & sectors will see huge inflows of cash. During the pandemic bounce in 2020, the work-from-home stocks, meme stocks, along with many tech & fintech stocks all went sky high. The fear of missing out (FOMO – it's a thing!) saw all kinds of money rushing into these stocks. I'm sure some clever traders made money but, less than two years later, many of those stocks have punished the gamblers & dreamers who were late jumping on the gravy train. And then didn't get off. We are all such sheep. Don't be a sheep.

Baa!

5. Don't Fear the Fees

This sounds contrary to everything I've said before, but it's not. Bear with me. If there was a fund that charged a 2% fee but that had a CAGR of 20% over the past decade or more, I'd be all over it for part of my portfolio. Yes, it's a high fee. But if the fund can consistently deliver that kind of return, after fees, I'm in. If you happen to know of such a fund, please message me!

The message I'm trying to get across here is that you shouldn't choose an ETF only on the basis of the fee charged. If the fund with a MER of 0.18% is consistently outperforming the one with the 0.06% MER, then it might be worth the extra cost. It just so happens that those are the MERs of XIU & XIC, both iShares® ETFs covering different areas of the Canadian market. Despite carrying the higher fee, XIU has outperformed over the past 10 years & with a little less volatility. Will it be the same going forward? Who knows. Along with the lower fee, there is a case to be made for the broader market coverage provided by XIC. Compared to the more limited coverage provided by XIU, which only holds 60 of the biggest companies trading on the Canadian market. Look outside the iShares® family & we find Vanguard Canada's VCE with a MER of 0.06% & a very slight outperformance over XIU. This ETF has fewer holdings than XIU, that adds risk, but it delivered a little extra reward in the recent past. It too is a good choice for some Canadian exposure. There are other Canadian

ETFs that offer similar performance, broadly similar sector exposure, & so on. Different investors choose differently, but all these ETFs are popular in Canada, so you'll have company whichever one you decide is right for your portfolio. You could probably pick from this selection of funds by throwing a dart & be just fine. That is not always the case, of course. And no, I am not suggesting that you use darts for stock or fund picking!

When it comes to actively managed funds, such as some high-income funds, the fees can go much higher. But it's still the relative performance, after fees, that matters. If the fund managers can consistently deliver superior performance, that can work. Depending on your goals, comparing results of such funds can take a little more work. Are you still accumulating via the DRIP, or are you spending the income? We might need to pay attention to the volatility metrics more now too. Look at the charts but also check out the volatility, best & worst years, biggest drawdowns, & so on. If long term income is the goal, check that the value of the fund grows when all the dividends & distributions are removed. Most of us would like to see both share price appreciation & income growth over time. Even if the total return doesn't match that of the market.

So, yes, fees matter. But the returns & the way those returns are delivered can matter more for some investors. Get used to comparing ETFs like this, it can make a difference.

6. Stop Whining

I hear a lot of people whining about big corporations getting rich at the expense of the little guy. Poor little me! As an investor you can drop that kind of talk. It doesn't matter what you do for your day job, once you become an investor you are now part of the corporate world. Profitability & shareholder return is now an important part of the equation for *you*. You want the corporations you own to be profitable. That's how you get rich.

Same thought strikes me when I hear people moaning about their cell phone bills, the price of gas, bank fees, & who knows what else. If you totally hate paying for something, but you continue to pay for it, you might want to consider buying some shares in the company. You'll stop whinging as soon as the first dividend dollars hit your account. I find myself trying to do business with companies that I'm invested in. There are companies that I feel "forced" to regularly do business with. Most of them might be in one of those index ETFs we talked about.

Of course, we all want to save money & pay less for our personal consumption needs. But just complaining doesn't help much. Instead, join the corporate world. As a shareholder, you're in business now. You can look at things differently.

Don't be a whiner, be a business owner.

7. Crypto

Crypto is pretty weird. It is a digital thing that is in limited supply. But it does nothing, produces nothing, & you can't buy anything with it during a grid outage. Will it work when the zombie apocalypse happens? Who's running this show? Nobody is not the right answer, there is always someone pulling stings. Someone is leveraging ignorance for gain. Crypto mining is energy intensive. It can't always be transacted quickly. And just what problem is this thing fixing? Why do we need it? My credit card or phone work just fine for online shopping or tapping.

I'm not saying the technologies surrounding crypto won't morph into something to be used by business, governments & financial institutions for managing the flow of wealth one day. And yes, I know there are reasons to not want government in our lives all the time. But in a democracy, our elected government is about all we've got as a backstop to dictatorial impulses, financial & otherwise. If there are companies that emerge from the crypo space that can get well paid for doing what they do, I might buy them when they can pay me a dividend. And when they are accountable. Right now, it feels like crypto investing is all about a bunch of people hoping it's worth something. They trade it back & forth in the hope that the next investor in line will pay them more than they bought it for.

I must admit, I was sucked in too. I bought one of the first crypto ETFs in Canada. I suddenly realised I had no idea what I was doing, no clue what it was worth, nor why I owned it. I sold it off for a little profit. I think I was lucky. Some would say I wasn't. Since it would be worth far more today had I kept it. Will it always be this way for crypto? I don't know. And I have absolutely no idea if I should have a little of it in my portfolio. But, for now, I don't.

Now that I think on it, crypto is not the strangest thing I ever heard of. Non-fungible tokens, or NFTs, are!

8. Bonds are Like Crypto

Bonds aren't really like crypto but let me tell you a story of my adventures in Brazil. Years ago, I travelled to South America for work. I loved going there & I tried to time my trips to escape from the Canadian winter for a couple or three weeks every year. Most of my trips included a visit to one of my favourite places on the planet, Manaus. A city of more than 2 million people, situated right on the banks of the mighty Amazon River. Yes, slap-bang in the middle of the rainforest. No way in or out but by boat or plane. And it's a long plane ride from the big cities.

The Brazilian government created a Free Tax Zone around Manaus to attract industry. That worked. Some of the largest companies I ever worked with were right there, amid the verdant jungle foliage. I loved going there. But it felt like there was a different currency on every trip. I experienced the cruzado, cruzeiro & real. Sometimes, one of the old currencies would have "nuvo" stuck in front to create the next one, as Brazil battled inflation with another new currency introduction. We're talking some heavy-duty inflation here. The factories I visited in Manaus were large compared to the Canadian factories I was familiar with. Here, it wasn't unusual for a facility to employ over ten thousand people. And there were a lot of factories packed into the industrial zone. During one of my trips, I saw what inflation could do. On pay day, most companies allowed their people to finish a little earlier than on other days of the week. The companies arranged for mobile bank branches to be on site so that employees could cash their cheques. The hordes of workers then boarded the huge fleet of buses & headed to the grocery store. Inflation was so rampant, they feared that if they didn't buy groceries on pay day, their money would buy far less on Monday. Now that's inflation!

During that same trip, you couldn't use credit cards. I had to take US dollar traveller's cheques instead. Checking out of the hotel at the end of that trip was a two-step process. Fortunately, my local colleague was on hand to assist. I needed his pockets! Since the hotel only took cash, we dashed off to the bank to trade my traveller's cheques for the cash to cover the bill. My colleague & I filled our pockets with several fist-sized rolls of bills & rushed back to the hotel to finalise the account. Those were crazy times. But I have loved Brazil since my very first trip & I look forward to getting back there again one day. They have that inflation thing under far better control now.

Aside from me enjoying the memories of my time in Brazil, there is a financial question here. What do you think would happen to bonds in such an inflationary environment? The paltry interest payment, which doesn't change for most bonds, wouldn't help much with the grocery shopping in such an inflationary environment. And the principle would buy a whole lot less at the end of the term too. This might work for the bond issuer. It would eradicate a lot of debt at lower cost. But for the bond holder, not so much. Under the wrong set of circumstances, bonds can be very risky.

How might crypto behave under such conditions? I'm asking, I really don't know.

Regardless of inflation, people will probably still clean their teeth. I wonder if owning shares in a toothpaste company might be a better option?

9. Emergency Fund

Aside from my a little of my personal paranoia being on display in the last chapter, a far more common nightmare is finding yourself in urgent need of cash & having none. We've touched on this a couple of times along the way, but it's important enough to warrant pulling all the threads together. It is really important to have an emergency fund in place **before** you start investing for wealth building. An emergency fund can reduce impact of what could be a financially catastrophic event. Losing a home due to job loss is near the top of the list of catastrophes. Aside from not having a place to live, that can screw up the wealth building process for years. Having an emergency fund to cover the rent or mortgage payments while you hunt down another job is critical.

The kind of work you do makes for different challenges too. Restaurant workers are usually very flexible & adaptable, for example. But then along comes covid & there are no restaurant jobs to be had. Who saw that one coming? The government covered things off for most of us this time around, will they do that next time? Employment Insurance will give employees some income if they are laid off, but the self-employed person might not have that protection. All such events scream out the need for having an emergency fund.

Everyone will have different needs with this. If you have a bus stop outside the front door, that car repair might not be as critical. A couple of higher income earners who live well within their means will worry less than the single person who must carry all the living costs based on one income. Having a family that can provide a financial crutch when needed is fantastic. But only if they can truly afford it. It's a bit like investing this, since we're trying to anticipate the unknown things that might come our way.

While imagining every possible situation is impossible, the bottom line is that it's important to have some immediately accessible cash to help offset the consequences of unforeseen events. Many of us worry about this kind of thing so, online, you'll find a lot of information on the permutations & combinations of disasters that you need to safeguard against. And there are online emergency fund calculators that will help you figure out how much you might need to stash away.

Use the same savings strategy we talked about to build up this fund. Automate the cash out of your spending account 'til you hit your target emergency amount & keep it in a high interest savings account that can be quickly accessed. If you can't max out your TFSA contribution room with long-term investments, it's a great idea to store some emergency funds here, tax free. Just don't allow that to undermine your long-term goals for the account.

While we should try to keep our investable money invested, there may come a time where you'll be glad you have a loaded TFSA to draw from. For an emergency that's just too big for your emergency fund to handle. While that might not have been the original intention behind investing inside the TFSA, if the emergency is big enough, the funds in your TFSA are available to stave off disaster. Load that TFSA truck up as soon as you can. It's like having an insurance policy that pays you while you wait for disaster to strike.

Emergency fund options might include some cash, but that gets evaporated by inflation. You could open a separate TFSA high interest saving account (HISA). Or you could buy some of the cash or HISA type ETFs inside your TFSA brokerage account. In April 2023, Horizons ETFs added another clever ETF to their stable: the Horizons 0-3 Month T-Bill ETF (CBIL). This is an ETF with about half a dozen short-term Government of Canada T-Bills that are continually replaced as the older ones mature. This ETF simplifies the T-Bill buying & diversification process for an individual investor. Though I usually shy away from new ETFs, this CBIL looks pretty cool. And about as safe as you can get for an investment. T-Bills are backed by the Canadian government. Though this ETF shows a yield, these T-Bills are not like bonds, where the underlying price can fluctuate. Instead, the T-Bills are purchased for less than face value & then mature at face value. With a T-Bill, your money can't go down. An ETF creates some additional bid-ask exposure & crazy things can happen with ETF trading, but this one looks pretty good. It currently pays a slightly lower yield than the HISA type ETFs, & T-bill rates can change, but it's still a potential option to keep your emergency fund growing. Especially with current interest rate levels in the 4 to 5% range. Though keeping pace with inflation is important, always keep some of your emergency fund in immediately accessible cash.

You can't trade some of these cash & savings type ETFs with all the big bank brokerages. Currently, I think CIBC Investor's Edge, Scotia iTrade & National Bank Direct Brokerage all let you trade them. Some of the other big bank brokerages, the ones that don't allow you to trade these ETFs, have their own HISA funds that you can buy instead. These are usually their own or partner products. The payout rates are a little less than some of the typical cash & HISA type ETFs, because of some internal fees charged. These in-house HISA funds have funny tickers, with letters & numbers, & they are usually traded on the mutual funds tab of the brokerage platform, rather than on the stock trading page. They might also take a little longer to have a trade settle, so your emergency funds might not be available for a day or two after you sell. While that seems all negative compared to the cash-like ETFs, some of these in-house HISA funds come with CDIC protection up to $100k. That's a cool feature that doesn't come with ETFs.

You could spread your emergency funds across two or three of these funds or ETFs, & across a couple of fund companies. Just in case anything weird happens right around the time your emergency strikes. Some cautious investors will even split their emergency funds across accounts at different financial institutions.

I hope you never need to use your emergency fund.

10. The Market is Risky

People worry a lot about their index ETFs, stocks, dividend security, & just about anything to do with their investments. No question, stocks can go down, dividends can be reduced & cut. That's why we put so much effort into trying to pick "good" stocks & funds. But try looking at it another way: imaging you are taking multiple part-time jobs at all the companies you buy shares in. Or at all those companies inside your ETFs.

In our early years, while up to our necks in mortgage payments, car loans, grocery bills & who knows what else, we depend on our paycheques to support us. A working couple is putting all its faith in two companies paying them enough cash to cover the bills. Maybe both partners have a part time job too. Okay, that's diversification across four companies.

You know where I'm going now, eh!

Having your money in a few ETFs containing hundreds, maybe thousands, of companies might actually be an improvement over the false sense of income security that comes with a day job.

If you've ever lost your job during a tough employment market, you know exactly what I mean.

11. Going for Growth

I know one kid who expects something on how to chase hot stocks, so this is the only hot-stock chapter in the entire book! Of course, rather than individual hot stocks, I will use a hot-stock index instead, the Nasdaq-100 Index®. This index contains 100 of the largest & most innovative stocks on the planet. If your buddies are trading hot stocks, chances are they'll be on the Nasdaq exchange. Because the US funds are older, I'm going to compare Invesco's QQQ to SPY this time. You'll find Canadian ETFs that cover both these indices, but the history isn't long enough for the story I'm about to tell you here.

And here is the short version of the story in a picture …

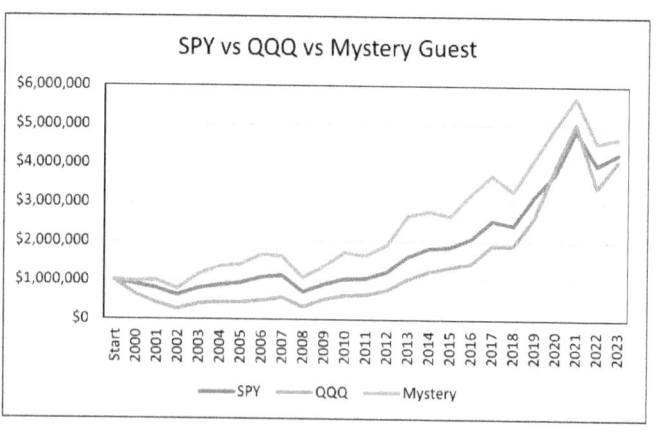

Fig. 6.11.1 SPY vs QQQ vs Mystery Guest since 2000

Younger investors might be surprised to see that there

isn't a huge difference in returns between the two over the past 23 years. In fact, the S&P 500® index is slightly ahead. I'm cheating a little here though, I started it right when the dot-com bubble burst, so the tech-heavy QQQ got hurt more back then. A lot of the innovation stocks were hammered at this time & recovery was slow. I see it this way because I was around back then. And I got burned back then.

Today's young investors may, however, see it like this …

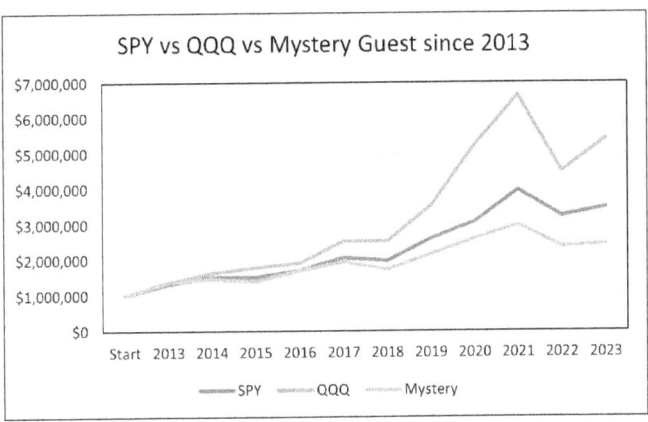

Fig. 6.11.2 SPY vs QQQ vs Mystery Guest since 2013

This is what the Nasdaq 100® is all about! It turned a million bucks into almost five & a half million in about ten years. It's crushing the old man's index now, eh! You were too young to pay attention to the market when the dot-com bubble burst & your experience with the Nasdaq-100 Index® is all about this kind of amazing growth. Younger investors might be subject to recency bias. Thinking that what's happened in recent times will continue to happen going forward. I got burned back in 2000, so I've got a longer-term view that has some pain associated with it. I know this index doesn't only go up. But, despite my painful memories, I still love the Nasdaq-100 Index®. If I was younger, I'd probably want some small holding of this baby in my portfolio. If you want to add some excitement to your life, there is nothing wrong with adding a little Nasdaq spice to your portfolio. But the story doesn't end there.

Look at the Mystery Guest. Did you notice that it beat both the indices in the first chart? That's the Russell 2000 Index®, a US small cap index managed by FTSE Russell, a subsidiary of the London Stock Exchange Group. If you're going to look at hot stuff, you might as well look at small caps too. It did the reverse of QQQ, performing better than the market over the longer period & worse over the most recent period. Recency bias might have a younger investor favouring QQQ over the small cap index fund. But if you recall the "reversion to the mean" thing, then that poor recent performance might mean that the small cap index will claw its way back into a leading position going forward. Does that make it a better contender for future growth?

Possibly. But you can see the dilemma with the whole past performance versus the future thing, the reversion to the mean thing, & jumping from one hot sector to the next. It's tough to guess what might happen next. There's an easier way to avoid all this guesswork. Own everything, so you've got some of whatever might be due for a hot streak. If you are investing in one of the all-equity funds (VEQT, XEQT, ZEQT), you've got everything in there, including the hot stocks & the small caps. Same thing with the all-in-one funds (VGRO, XGRO, ZGRO). Along with the bond ballast in these funds, you've got that same global markets & diverse market cap exposure.

One of the lessons to be learned from these chart comparisons is the length of time it takes for some of these things to play out. We're mentally wired to think in far shorter timeframes. But some of this stuff works its way through market cycles that span decades. Excruciating, eh?

But if you want to speculate with a very small allocation to something exciting along the way, several companies, including BMO, Blackrock, Horizons & Invesco, all offer Canadian-listed ETFs that track the Nasdaq-100 Index®. Choices are more limited for Canadian-listed offerings that cover the Russell 2000 Index®. Blackrock's iShares® U.S. Small Cap Index ETF, ticker XSU, is a Canadian dollar hedged fund that does this. There are some interesting, factor-biased small cap funds trading on the US exchanges, if you want to explore a bit. Just remember that the less you know, the broader you go, especially with your core holdings. Those globally diversified funds will have a little of everything inside.

12. Investor Behaviour

If you really get into this whole investing thing, you will likely become exposed to some additional risk. Starting out, it's very easy to buy into a broad index strategy & start rolling. Only to then see another strategy outperforming yours. Just like we saw in the last chapter. There will be times where the simple, indexing strategy won't be on top. As you continue to learn, your appreciation for different strategies will increase. But you may find yourself buying into a new strategy too soon. Or too late. Or you'll find your old strategy starts working well again. Right after you dropped it!

There will be times where one or another approach will outperform the market. One day it will look like momentum investing is the way to go. Next year perhaps a value strategy might take over. It could be some other factor or strategy that will lead the pack during the next cycle. There are times when new, hot strategies become all the rage. Or old ones bloom again. This is usually a temporary condition. Many investors who chase the current hot stocks, sectors, factors, or strategies tend to underperform the market. For DIY investors, changing strategies is like trying to time the market. Most of us aren't any good at that & jumping from one strategy to another on a regular basis can lead to underperformance.

This is not to say that you shouldn't test drive other strategies. But it might be better to test anything outside of your current strategy in a play portfolio first.

Or you could start an entirely separate portfolio that follows a different strategy to your primary portfolio. It's not unusual for investors to run multiple strategies. Or to use a hybrid approach. But you might not want to sell off the old one in favour of the new one every time you want to try something new. Unless you chose a total dog, let it ride!

Even with commitment to a particular strategy, it's possible to make mistakes. When I was an avid follower of the dividend growth strategy, for example, I was all in & I pursued that strategy to the max. Including in my cash account. Coming up to tax reporting time, I suddenly realised that I had added unnecessary tax liability because of my choices. Despite my love of dividends, one of the Horizon's total return ETFs might have been a far better choice in a taxable account. It would have delivered on performance, but without taxable distributions. The dividends would have been captured inside the ETF & taxes would have been deferred until I sold shares. And any gains from selling shares would be treated more favourably as capital gains.

In general, it's probably a good idea to not chase whatever is already hot. If everyone thinks it's hot today, it might not be so hot tomorrow. Investors who chop & change regularly tend to underperform regularly. Over the long haul, you might do better picking a broadly diversified strategy & sticking with it.

13. Who Really Knows?

Investing is a bit like hockey. You'll hear a bunch of guys sitting around talking hockey over a beer & some of them can't even skate. Ironically, the guy who can't skate sometimes picks the winner. Anyone can talk about investing too. It's pretty easy to sound smart, especially to the uninitiated, when it comes to investing. Toss in a few investy-sounding buzzwords, quote a few lines from some famous investing geniuses, & you can sound like you know what you're talking about. Join some online groups & you'll find them filled with experts parroting some line they read or heard about from another online expert. But how can you filter this? Where do you draw the line on qualifying someone as an expert? How much do we need to know in order to assess the expertise of another?

I follow a bunch of real experts online. How do I know they are real? I don't really. Because I don't know enough to assess the quality of their knowledge. I might need to know more than they do, in order to pass judgment on their knowledge. And I don't. But I'm guessing they're real because they do some sophisticated analysis that is well beyond my ability. That impresses me. Some of them manage money & run funds. I've followed a few that really impressed me & then I looked at the funds they managed. Some of them were underperforming the market consistently. That was a bit of a shocker. Maybe their strategies will work better over longer timeframes, I don't know. Market indices have historical data to support that approach, is there any point in following the advice of someone who can't match that?

These experts may be a whole lot smarter & more educated but, at the end of the day, they're doing the same thing we're doing. We're all trying to figure out what happens next. The reason we all invest, idiot & expert alike, is because the markets have grown over time. Through wars, natural disasters, financial catastrophes, & pandemics, the markets have always recovered & grown. While every expert out there will cite the line about past performance not being a guarantee of future results, that's really what we're all betting on, isn't it? We're betting that the markets will continue to grow in the future. Because they have in the past. If the markets didn't have a history of consistent growth, we'd all be looking for something else to invest in. When you think about what's going on here, it seems like we're all going for it based on faith & hope, & in ignorance of what the future holds. But the reality is that none of us knows what happens next. Is it possible that this ongoing ever-upward trend will stop one day? You'd have to think it is. Ask a dinosaur. I'm just hoping in doesn't happen in our lifetimes. Or we're back to the best investment being that wilderness farm with a fishing pond again.

14. ESG

Some of the goals of ESG create a conflict in my mind. I'm all for saving the planet for you kids. But, with only a hint of guilt attached, I'm also very interested in maximising my financial comfort in retirement.

I'm not a hard-core tree-hugger but I do try to do a little bit for the environment. I recycle properly & I try to pick up three pieces of plastic every time I visit a beach. I'm sure I'll buy an electric car one day, though I'm not ready just yet. I've seen Canadian governments spend my tax dollars on green initiatives. Only to see some of those investments move to other countries when subsidies dry up. It feels like there are forty shades of green in this whole ESG space. Of course, ESG is now part of the marketing toolkit in the investment industry. Outside the colour of money, marketing is not inherently green. I'll continue to learn as I go. But I'm also happily invested in traditional Canadian energy companies. Oil is a fossil fuel, after all. That makes it sound so earthy, so green, eh!

As energy companies go, I think Canadian energy companies are about as green as the fossil fuel industry gets. While I acknowledge it's a pretty pale shade of green, they also employ a lot of people & they pay taxes. Taxes that might help recover some of the money that was spent on those green initiatives. And those fossil fuel taxes will support future green initiatives. It's a bit of a devil's pact but, to drag out another old saying: it might be that it's better the devil you know!

While I don't mind investing in energy companies, I would not want to invest in a business that condoned issues of race, gender, child labour, & so on. Those should be the minimum expectations we have for all our businesses. The tragedy here is that we feel the need to specifically identify such failings under an ESG banner. Everyone must make their own choice with this. It's a difficult area to navigate. When it comes to buying ESG funds, make sure you are doing what you intend. And try to look behind the marketing messages that you will hear. Marketing is less about educating us. And more about selling a product at a profit. Putting green in the name or ESG in the title doesn't automatically make for a good investment. And, sometimes, the product might not be as ESG-friendly as we would like.

I have one big regret in this entire space. If only I had invested all my cigarette money in the stocks of the cigarette companies!

15. What if You Don't Have Enough?

If you don't have enough to retire on, you can't retire. I wish there was a magic wand to fix this for you but there isn't. I am pained just imagining how awful it must be to reach 65 & to feel forced to continue working at a job you no longer want to do. But what else can you do? Forego CPP up to age 70 & you can increase your CPP payments by 42%. Pass on OAS payments at 65 & you'll have a 36% increase by age 70. But you need income all the way to age 70 to do that. What if you don't have it?

The world is an unforgiving place sometimes. If you don't save & invest far enough ahead of retirement, you might be faced with such pain. I'm sorry, I don't know what else to tell you.

If you are young, you know what you need to do to avoid this happening to you later in life. Don't keep putting it off.

16. Things to do When I Die

This one is one my To-Do list!

I think you can claim a small CPP death benefit. And maybe there's some death coverage on those credit cards? Oh, those need to be cancelled too, eh! Did I keep up with that old insurance policy or not? Who's going to manage the will & any leftovers that might be in the portfolio by then? Do I need a new will?

Wow, is that all I know? Seems like I'm way behind with my end-of-life planning & prep work. It'll be difficult to recover from this one if I miss the **dead**line!

I'm **dying** laughing as I write here! LOLOL

Okay, okay, I'm going to prioritise this one now. Maybe you can get this to-do done earlier than I have.

17. Making Too Much Money

This one comes up every now & then, so it's worth a quick mention. It is not true that you'll take home less than you used to if you get a raise or a bonus that bumps you into a higher tax bracket. We have a tiered tax system in Canada. As you earn more, you can be pushed into a higher tax band, & your tax rate does go up. It only goes up on the extra bit of the income that falls into the higher tax band. It does not work its way back down to the lower amounts we were already earning in the lower tax bands. We do not pay more tax on the amounts we were earning before.

This means that you *always* want more money. You always want that pay increase, that bonus, & more paid overtime. The government takes a little more tax from each new dollar you're earning at the higher tax rate, but you still have more money in your pocket at the end of the day. Outside of potential exposure to losing qualification for some other government subsidies or benefits, you never turn down the opportunity to earn more!

18. Fun Numbers

Here are some fun numbers to keep in mind as you go though the daily grind.

The Rule of 72
The Rule of 72 is a quick way to calculate how long it takes your money to double at a given rate of annual return. It's not perfectly accurate, but it's close enough for fun coffee conversations. Divide 72 by the annual rate of return to see how long it will take your money to double. An investment that returns 10% annually will double in 7.2 years. A 7.2% return will get you a double in 10 years. Pop quiz: how long will it take your money to double at a 9% rate of return?

Know Your OC Number
A 20-year-old investing $10 today, at 10%, will see that grow to about $850 by retirement day. A 35-year-old only has 30 years to retirement. That means that same $10 could become $193 for this investor. Your personal OC Number is the Opportunity Cost of spending, rather than investing, that $10 today. Use a compound growth calculator to get your personal OC Number. Keep that $10 OC Number in your head. Now you have an easy way to do a little mental arithmetic when you're trying to decide between saving & spending. That thousand-dollar thingy will cost me $85k by retirement day? Eek! No thanks!

Your Duck Me Number
Your Duck Me Number is your financial freedom

portfolio size. Once you've grown a portfolio that can deliver enough income with the 4% rule, or with a 4% dividend yield, you can smile & say ... Duck me, I'm free! It'll take a bit of time, but it is something to look forward to.

Double Double Your Money

The Rule of 72 is only half the numbers story. If I asked you to work a whole day for me, for just a penny, would you? Probably not, eh!

Guess how much I'd owe you if I asked you to work a whole month for me, but this time I offer you a penny the first day & I promise to double your money every day for the next 30 days? Don't take me up on it, there are 30 doubles in there & I'd owe you about $21.5 million at the end of the month. And there's no way I could afford to pay you! LOL

CAGR is the King of Numbers

Compounding returns create exponential growth. Our portfolio gets bigger, faster, over time. And that's why all the really exciting stuff happens in a portfolio as you get closer to retirement. You just need to start early & give it enough time. More time allows for more doubles. The later doubles are worth far more. Use apps & online tools that show you the CAGR of your investments. We don't do CAGR well in our heads. It's not yield, it's not dividend-growth, or any other number. While all those contribute to the result, CAGR is the King of Numbers when comparing investment performance.

19. What Did I Tell My Kids?

I worried about putting this chapter in, but I finally decided it would be unfair not to. Please be aware that this is not financial or investment advice & it particularly is not for **you**! But it shows how my real world works & that reality is sometimes a little messier than the plan.

The background is I totally messed up my kids before I pulled my thoughts together on all this. My early suggestion to them was to buy the American & Canadian index funds. I would occasionally mention a dividend-growth stock that I felt was currently undervalued. I tripped them up from time to time by telling them that the market was overvalued & that they should park the cash & wait 'til the market dropped. How bad a Dad am I, eh? Teaching them to try to time the market! And yes, it was bad advice. All I did in the early stages was create confusion for them. To be honest, I'm not sure how often they ignored me!

When I eventually got around to going through it all for them, I suggested they open an RBC InvestEase® account. And to stick a few hundred bucks into whatever robo-advised portfolio that was offered after they answered all the questions. Then they could just watch it for a few years to see what happens. Why that approach & that robo-advisor?

Well, for starters, it meant that they could put off learning about DIY investing & comparing a bunch of brokerages & ETFs. I didn't want them to put off doing that, but I knew it could easily happen. They're busy building their young lives & that can be far more exciting than learning about all this investing stuff. Comparing robo-advisors would have been another excuse to delay getting started, so I just picked one. I should have done the comparisons for them, but I had other things to worry about at the time & I didn't. I'm pretty sure any of the other robo-advisors would work well too. But RBC is Canada's biggest bank & it's been around for more than a century & a half, so I took the lazy path. This robo-advisory service comes with real humans that you can email & call. You only need a hundred bucks to get started. I felt this was a fast & simple approach that would help them get going. You can also fully automate the saving & investing process with an account like this. You know how important that is now.

I told them to only put in some money that they could afford to lose. I wasn't expecting them to lose it, I just didn't want them learning to invest with cash they might need to yank back out in the next couple of years. The robo-advisory fee is 0.5% & the average basket of ETF fees might be around 0.2%, give or take, for a total fee drag of about 0.7%. The allocations are all RBC iShares® ETFs. BlackRock & RBC have a working relationship for the iShares® products. I thought that might help eliminate any dithering over who had the "best" index funds for each market. Sometimes, having less choice works better!

When they get around to learning more, or if they open self-directed accounts, they can just copy the asset allocations from their robo-account. Or buy an all-in-one ETF that gets somewhere close to the robo-advisor's asset allocation model. That would save them the 0.5% fee going forward. But they could keep the original robo-account too. With that dual pronged approach, they would still have access to the advice in the robo-account. Advice that could then be applied to the DIY account, only at lower cost.

So what do you think my kids did afterwards?

I have no idea. But I'm pretty sure it's not this.

Dad's are used to being ignored! LOL

20. What's Wrong What I Told My Kids?

Not too much, I think. Before I suggested that approach for them, I back tested a breakdown of XEQT & VGRO against VFV & a portfolio of 20 Canadian dividend stocks. The dividend portfolio was a mix of banks, telcos, energy, & a few others that you'd find in the typical Canadian's dividend portfolio. I just grabbed them out of my head, from a list of stocks that I owned, or wanted to own, previously.

With all dividends & distributions reinvested, here are the results …

Portfolio	CAGR
Canadian Dividend 20	12.2%
XEQT Breakdown	8.9%
VGRO Breakdown	6.8%
Vanguard S&P 500 Index ETF	11.1%

6.20.1 Portfolio Returns from 2016-01 to 2022-08

Why would I want my kids to have a portfolio that produces less than the Canadian Dividend 20 or the even simpler S&P 500 Index® ETF? The returns on the all-equity & all-in-one funds are way lower.

I preferred those more diversified funds for them because I don't know what happens next. I don't know how much time they would dedicate to monitoring & rebalancing their portfolio of individual stocks. I know they don't have the time to spend on learning how to manage a stock portfolio today. The US market has been a winner over international markets for decades now. Why not just use that?

Because I don't know what will happen with that index either. What if there's another lost decade in the works? The more globally diversified funds might outperform if international markets have a period of outperformance over the American market. Is that possible?

I don't know the answers to any of those questions. My crystal ball is still broken.

I thought the broader diversity might protect them. The narrower the focus of a portfolio, the greater the potential for volatility. While the greater diversification may limit upside, it may also help with limiting the downside. I figured that the greater diversity might serve them better 'til they can make the time to figure it all out for themselves. The more important thing for me was to give them something simple to get started with. Not getting started is probably the bigger mistake. And it's the one many of us fall foul of.

Of course, my personal conservative biases are built into this thinking & I worry more about losing my kids' money than I do my own. I can only hope I don't get it too wrong for them!

21. What Now?

If you're new to investing & you made it this far, great! But it's not enough. Adding action items to your to-do list is not enough. You need to DO something now. No matter how little you can afford, automate your saving & investing process right away. Pick a simple strategy & get started. It's too easy to put things off. The longer you put this off, the greater the lost opportunity cost. Even if you start out with very little, somewhere down the road, it might be 5, 10, or even 15 years from now, I hope you'll look at your portfolio & see that time can work magic. And if everything works out, you might be far better prepared for retirement than the average Canadian. I wish I had done this when I was your age.

If you are totally stuck & can't decide what to do, please go see an advisor. They will help get you started. If you already have an advisor & some savings, go have a chat about the strategy being used. You should be in a better position to get value from that conversation now. Despite the extra costs involved with paying for advice, if it gets you going, it may be worth it.

Whatever you decide to do, whatever investing choices you make, I hope it all works out for you. I hope you will achieve financial freedom your way & that you'll get to enjoy more hours on those white sandy beaches down the road.

Have a safe & profitable journey, guys, I wish you all the very best on your path through life.

Paul

PS ... The reason there's a cute little duck on the front cover is because I couldn't draw a cute little Canada goose!

And I use the little duck as the icon at my website & blog. I blog about this stuff at www.TheWryEye.com

www.ingramcontent.com/pod-product-compliance
Lightning Source LLC
Chambersburg PA
CBHW070528220526
45467CB00003B/898